FOLK MUSIC
IN THE
UNITED STATES

FOLK MUSIC IN THE UNITED STATES

an introduction

by **BRUNO NETTL**
UNIVERSITY OF ILLINOIS at Urbana-Champaign

Third Edition, revised and expanded by HELEN MYERS
COLUMBIA UNIVERSITY

Wayne State University Press
Detroit, 1976

First edition, *An Introduction to Folk Music in the United States*, copyright © 1960 by Wayne State University Press. Second edition, rev., © 1962; reprinted 1965, 1974.

Library of Congress Cataloging in Publication Data

Nettl, Bruno, 1930–
  Folk music in the United States.

  Previous editions published under title: An introduction to folk music in the United States.
  Includes bibliographical references.
  Includes index.
  1. Folk music—United States.   I. Myers, Helen, 1946–   II. Title.
ML3551.N47   1976   781.7'73   76–84
ISBN 0-8143-1556-9
ISBN 0-8143-1557-7 pbk.

I hear America singing, the varied carols I hear.

Walt Whitman
Leaves of Grass

CONTENTS

LIST OF MUSICAL EXAMPLES

PREFACE

Folk music has become such a popular subject in the United States that hundreds of collections, printed and recorded, and dozens of descriptive books have appeared. Most of the latter concern themselves with specific and special fields within American folk music but, perhaps surprisingly, no over-all survey of the subject in its entirety exists. This volume is intended, in an introductory and elementary fashion, to fill that gap. It does not pretend to be definitive or comprehensive nor to present new material. Based largely on the extant literature of the field, its purpose is to introduce the layman and the student to the great variety of forms, styles, and cultures represented in the folk music of this country. Besides the Anglo-American heritage, we deal with Afro-American and American Indian cultures, with the folk music of rural non-English-speaking minorities, and with folk music in the city. Of course, only a glimpse into each of the larger categories can be offered, and many important song types, instruments, and, indeed, ethnic groups had to be omitted for lack of information or space. The emphasis is on cultural background and context, and on the music; the words of songs are here a secondary consideration. We have tried to include such information on folk music in general as is necessary for understanding the material in this country (hence the non-American examples), and we have gone slightly beyond what is usually included in discussions of folk music in order to show its use in the modern city, in the professional folk singer's repertory, and in art or cultivated music. I should like to stress the introductory character of this presentation, and to advise the reader to continue further into the fascinating world of folk music and folk song, a world to which the United States makes a unique contribution. The chapter bibliographies are included with the reader's further exploration in mind.

It is twenty years since this modest attempt to give an overview of the folk music—or, rather, folk *musics*—of the United States was first written, and fifteen years since it was published. Folk music itself has changed since that time; it has had a role in the recent history of this country. More important, our understanding of folk music as a concept, as a group of musical repertories, as a kind of music which interacts with other musics extant in the world, as the expression of culture and human behavior, has changed greatly, presumably becoming more sophisticated, through the rapid development of the field of ethnomusicology. It seems appropriate now to provide a thoroughly revised edition which takes into account at least some of these changes. We thus present a substantially new version of *An Introduction to Folk Music in the United States*.

The work of revising has been in essence and substance the work of Helen Myers, who has greatly expanded the chapters on Afro-American and urban folk musics and written an entirely new chapter on Hispanic-American folk music. She has also brought other parts of the book up to date, emphasizing new approaches to research, collecting, and understanding, and has included some of the results of her field research in the folk music culture of New York City.

Bibliographies have been updated, all chapters have been
thoroughly rewritten, and their order has been changed to
facilitate smoother reading. In other respects, however, the
basic structure, approaches, and attitudes expressed in the
first two editions of my *Introduction to Folk Music in the
United States* remain intact.

Bruno Nettl
July 1975

I

INTRODUCTION

For centuries it has been said that folk music is dying. English and German collectors of the nineteenth century were already engaged in what they thought was a salvage operation, and many professional folklorists and ethnomusicologists have long considered preservation their main task. Generations of scholars and teachers in the United States have forecast the end of American folk music, fearing that modernization, the breakdown of rural society, and the coming of mass media were bound to homogenize the musical culture of this nation. But American folk music did not die. Today, as the United States begins her third century of nationhood, this country remains unusually rich in folk music.

Folk music is often thought of as the expression of a people, or a national or ethnic group, and in many ways this is a valid definition. We know that a folk song, even though composed by a member of a given ethnic group, will not take hold in that group unless it conforms to the current aesthetic ideals. It may be rejected, or it may be accepted and then changed through the process of communal re-creation until it does conform. Consequently, the music of an ethnic group tends to be homogeneous and to express in some ways the character of that people. In Europe and other parts of the Old World where most groups have had long continuous residence in the same geographical area, folklore is rooted in the soil and in the history.

Folk music in the United States reflects the history and composition of American society. It stands as a testament to the diverse cultures of millions of immigrants who have crossed the Atlantic to the New World. The trademark of American folk music, therefore, is variety. At its roots is an English folk song tradition that has been modified to suit the specific requirements of America. An important stream of African culture, introduced by the Black slaves, has interacted with this Anglo-American tradition since the seventeenth century. In the nineteenth century, immigrants from many European countries—Germany, France, Italy, Greece, Poland, Czechoslovakia, Russia, the Ukraine—added their various musics to the amalgam. Immigrants from Asia, the Caribbean, and South America have contributed other musical styles to the American cultural mosaic. Underneath these various layers of European, African, Asian, and Latin American musics lies a relatively uninfluential but significant force— the culture of the American Indian. If we restricted the concept of a nation's folk music to the creations of that country's indigenous inhabitants, this American Indian music would be our only genuine tradition. But ironically, most Americans do not regard Indian music as a part of their experience, nor do they understand it. We may conclude that many borrowed, nonindigenous traditions are the basis for most folk music in the United States. It is the mixing and blending of these that is characteristically American.

As the proportion of immigrants from various European and Asian countries has changed periodically, the ethnic composition of the United States and the complexion of its culture have also changed. In the middle of the nineteenth century, the heavy influx of Germans gave a special flavor to American folk music. This was altered as many immigrants from Ireland, Italy, and eastern Europe followed. After the arrival of these groups, their continued flux from one region to another, the rapid urbanization of some districts and the isolation of others, shaped the development of American civilization.

The United States has always been composed of combinations of ethnic groups, a situation that also occurs in European countries but in different ways. In Europe, if several ethnic groups live in a nation, they are usually relatively isolated from one another. In Czechoslovakia, for example, the Czech- and German-speaking inhabitants had little contact, except among intellectuals. Even in Switzerland, the German, French, and Italian groups have their own traditions, and share little common folklore.

In the United States, however, the various ethnic groups have tended to mix. America has no long tradition of cultural integrity, and practical considerations favored minorities becoming at least partially incorporated into the Anglo-American community. The German-American takes part in the traditions of both Germany and America, the Ukrainian-American in those of his homeland and the United States. A few enclaves of Europeans, to be sure, preserve their old culture almost intact. But the majority of ethnic groups in America participate in a combination of traditions. The Italian-American may associate with his countrymen from Italy in church and in social clubs, but on the job he is likely to come in contact with members of many other ethnic groups. When he listens to the radio, watches television, reads the newspaper and magazines, he is exposed to mainstream American culture. The United States, then, is a vast system of interlocking, interacting ethnic networks, superimposed on a basic Anglo-American cultural foundation. Thus, the experiences of the Czech-American are quite different from those of the Czech, and Italian-American folklore is quite different from its Italian counterpart, in form and content. Although almost all bodies of folklore in the world are represented in America, in making the transition they have sometimes lost their original functions. Harvesting songs from Yugoslavia are not used for harvest here because the Yugoslavs in America are rarely farmers. A musical style used in Africa for paddling songs (see Example 22) is used in America for entertainment.

Our polyglot heritage and our hybrid culture have led some to ask: is there a genuinely American folklore? Let us simply state that American folk music is a very different phenomenon from its European counterpart, but the differences between American and European folk music may be explained by the different historical developments and contrasting cultural composition of the two hemispheres. Both continents have a heritage that can be considered genuine folklore.

Unlike European folk culture, which dates back more than a thousand years, America's folklore is young. The colonial period of the seventeenth century is the starting point for American traditions, marking the transplantation of European cultures to the eastern seaboard and the first contact between Whites and American Indians. The phenomenon of the frontier is also uniquely American. During the nineteenth century, as new European immigrants poured into the eastern United States, descendants of the original colonists began the push westward from the Appalachians to the Pacific. As the great folk myth of the West emerged in the mid-1800's, the nation was torn by the slavery question and civil war. Each of these events shaped the emerging folk culture and each was celebrated in folk tale and folk song.

Today the United States, more than Europe, is largely an urban country, a situation that has raised many questions for scholars of folk music, particularly in the last few decades. In most European countries, especially those in the eastern, central, and southern parts of the continent, the difference between urban and rural populations is considerable. But in the United States rural inhabitants share many of the urban cultural features, such as radio and television, newspapers and nationally circulated magazines, motion pictures, machinery, and mechanical devices. In contrast to most of Europe, the American rural population is quite mobile. People travel in automobiles much more than in Europe, and the migration between farm and city is steady and strong. There are relatively few individuals who have never lived in a city. Consequently we cannot, in this country, consider a rural environment as the chief feature of folk music—as students of European folklore have often done. American folk music lives in the city. It thrives, even in the large urban areas. It is especially conspicuous where European or Asian minorities have settled in industrial centers and retained parts of their heritage. But these ethnic enclaves are certainly not the only examples of urban folk music.

Unlike Europe, America has been the setting for the contact of a large European population with two non-European, non-White groups—the Black Africans and the American Indians. These two situations provide contrasting examples for the student of culture contact or *acculturation*. The American Indian, pushed back by the westward surge, has always lived on the fringes of American civilization. The Black, on the other hand, has been in the mainstream of American life since the earliest days of slavery. Afro-American music is the child of an Anglo-American and an African folk music tradition. These two styles have blended to produce today's Black music, which bears resemblance to both parents but is a truly unique phenomenon. American Indian music, however, has only in exceptional cases blended with the Anglo-American folk tradition. Today's American Indian has "compartmentalized" his repertory. He knows American songs and he knows Indian songs, but he does not mix or confuse the two.

The mixed ethnic background of the American community and the urban make-up of American society make this country an ideal setting for the study of acculturation. Ethnic minorities have adapted to the United States in various ways.

Some groups have become absorbed in the mainstream of American life, while others, such as the Amish, remain isolated. The Amish, a Swiss-German farmer group, who sing hymns in a style very different from almost anything else in American or European folklore—a style that seems distantly related to sixteenth- and seventeenth-century German cultivated music—are an example of the theory of *marginal survivals,* which demonstrates how a trait may disappear in the original center of its geographic distribution (Germany and Switzerland in this case) but can survive and even flourish much longer in the outskirts or margins of that area (in this case among German-Americans).

This theory also helps to account for the great wealth of European folk music in America, a wealth which makes it possible, at least in some ways, to study at first hand the folk songs of most Old World cultures without leaving the United States. The United States is fertile soil for studying British folklore, and European folk song collectors have often come to America to round out knowledge of their native traditions. They often find that America has preserved a great deal of European folklore which has disappeared in its original home. In 1916, Cecil J. Sharp, a noted English folk song scholar, heard that the old English and Scottish ballads were still being sung in the United States. His field trip to the mountain areas of Virginia, North Carolina, Tennessee, and Kentucky showed that the number of variants of these ballads current among the folk far exceeded that of present-day Britain; and he discovered some songs that had died out in British folk tradition.

The American scene offers a great challenge to the student of folk music. Opportunities are presented to study the effects of culture contact on music and the role of music in the adaptation of minority groups to the larger community. Old World musical cultures may be studied in America. The survival of Africanisms may be explored in the music of Black Americans. America preserves marginal survivals— traditions like those of the Amish. The number of diverse folk musics in this country is probably unmatched by any other nation, and the number of scholarly problems presented by this material is limitless. Moreover, American folk music is constantly changing. As immigrants continue to arrive, new traditions are introduced. Some older groups are gradually forgetting their heritage and becoming assimilated into the Anglo-American culture. Others are consciously trying to revive old customs and folkways. Increasingly, ethnic minorities regard their own folk music as a prime symbol of group unity and of ethnicity. Often the grandchildren of immigrants take pride in learning the language of the old country—in many cases a language the fathers and mothers had forgotten.

The hegemony of the mass media has made the dissemination of folk music possible, permitting ethnic minorities to broadcast their cultural forms to the larger American community. The mass media have led to the recent popularization of many folk styles—country western music, for instance, and so-called "hillbilly" music. Because of the mass media, no doubt the musical experience of many if not most Americans today is essentially the same; but at the same time, the experience of the individual has broadened and diversified. We perhaps no longer have many persons who listen to only one kind of music; most are involved in the total musical culture of the nation. But each person still has a type of music that he considers uniquely his own and the special symbol of his population group. In many cases the nature of this music and the ways it is transmitted challenge the older definitions of folk music—a question which must be raised in the following chapter. But folk music is still very much alive in America today.

II

DEFINING FOLK MUSIC

The term "folk music" has been much used and abused in recent years, but it has been endowed with ever-increasing prestige. Much misuse of the term has been caused by a new veneration for folk music by the public, a veneration that has been exploited by those who have found that their sales increase when "folk" is put on the label. Consequently, the term has often been used to identify music which under no honest definition could be accepted as folklore. Some confusion has indirectly stemmed from the failure of scholars to agree on a generally accepted definition;[1] and because of this confusion some choose to avoid the issue, and have stopped using the term "folk music" entirely.

Folk music is a particularly difficult concept to define because its style, cultural function, and relationship to other types of music have varied considerably during different periods of Western history. Moreover, different cultures have their own ways of categorizing folk music: what is typical of folk music in Europe or America may not be typical of folk music in India or Japan. In the past, scholars of Western music have used two main approaches. The one took the stylistic features of the music itself as the important criteria and the other the music's cultural milieu or background. For some people, folk music had to sound a certain way and had to be composed in a particular style. For others, folk music was all music produced by that group in society defined as the "folk."

Folklorists have had considerable difficulty deciding who the "folk" are, and nothing is better evidence of their lack of unanimity than the many definitions in the *Standard Dictionary of Folklore*.[2] Students of music have also used many definitions of "folk" and folk music. For Béla Bartók, folk music was simply peasant music, or rural music:[3] For some scholars it has meant the characteristic music of a country or ethnic group, whether rural or urban. Who the folk are is constantly changing. Today, with the proliferation of mass media, modern technology, and easy mobility, the isolated rural peasant enclaves have largely vanished, especially in the United States. Most modern researchers tend to believe that folk music exists today and has existed in the past in the towns and cities as well as in rural areas.

Part of the problem of defining folk music is the popular notion that all folklore must be very old. A common feature in the creation myths of many nonliterate tribes is the idea that their songs have always been with their people. Scholars have tended to emphasize such traditions, and often rejected folk material as not "genuine" because it apparently lacked sufficient age. But, while a style may be very old, the songs composed in that style may be comparatively recent. We must, therefore, distinguish between individual creations and the style in which they are composed. Many folk songs are only a few decades old, others are somewhat older, and some may even go back centuries. Some new folk songs are not appreciably different in style from old folk songs. The opposite may also be true, however. A song may be old, but it may have changed in style over the years so that it bears hardly any evidence of its age. All of this shows us that, in contrast to cultivated music (music that is part of a culture through a written tradition), a folk song often has a life quite independent of its characteristic qualities which we call "style."

Western scholars have often maintained that the origin of a piece of music determines whether it is folklore or not. For some, a song composed by a trained, professional composer is not acceptable as folk music, but one created by an untrained musician is acceptable. Then again, we find the opinion that a song is a folk song even if written by a trained composer, so long as its origin is not known to the performers and hearers. The trouble with these definitions, however valuable in special cases, is that they depend on the gaps in our knowledge of folk song origins; if our information increases, the number of folk songs would have to decrease. Although a song may not have changed, if its origin is discovered, it would have to be reclassified.

Another basis for defining folk music is the manner in which it is transmitted. People learn some things through reading and other things by being told or shown. News read in a newspaper and a skill learned from a textbook are elements of culture transmitted in written tradition. Information passed from one person to another through speech is transmitted in oral tradition; songs, tales, beliefs, proverbs, riddles, methods of sewing, decorating, boat-building may be transmitted in this way and, if so, are classed as folklore. Some cultures, like those of the American Indians, the sub-Saharan Africans, and the Polynesians, until recently used oral tradition almost exclusively. But the members of urban cultures, living in the centers of literate societies, also learn much by oral tradition, directly from other people, perhaps from their parents and friends. Music transmitted through oral tradition has generally been accepted by scholars as folklore, and oral tradition is the most commonly accepted criterion of folk music today.

School songs and religious music are often passed on by oral tradition, but few scholars have classified them as folklore, for they are associated with institutions like schools and churches, and they are composed, written, taught, and developed by professional musicians. Hymns and songs taught in school are usually passed on by means of printed media, and oral tradition enters only when a large mass of people learn them. On the other hand, some hymns do live entirely or largely in oral tradition, and these are distinguished by the term "folk hymn."

A song may be considered a folk song at one time or in one place and an art song at a different time or place. Many songs begin in written form, created by a trained composer, and remain in the art song tradition. If, at the same time, they pass into the oral tradition, they can also be considered folk songs.

How and why does folk music come into being? This has been answered in many ways by many scholars. An early theory, propounded among others by the famous Grimm brothers, proposes that all folklore, including folk music, is the expression of an entire people and that the whole ethnic group is the creator of each item of folklore.[4] While this theory of the communal origin of folklore is credible in a rather indefinite and idealistic sense, it does not give due credit to the individual creators of folklore; indeed, this theory does not recognize them at all, and it is hardly accepted today.

Another theory, maintained by the Germans Hans Naumann and John Meier, and slightly related to—but also distinct from—that of communal creation, states that an item of folklore, such as a song, originates in a sophisticated, urban society as art music, and is later taken up by lower social strata. It becomes *gesunkenes Kulturgut* (a debased or lowered cultural element).[5] For example, some songs by Franz Schubert, a member of a sophisticated musical culture, have passed into oral tradition and become folk songs in Austria and southern Germany. On the other hand, this theory does not admit that folklore and folk music could be created by the members of folk cultures. Like communal creation, it does not credit the individual in a folk community with creativity.

The relationship between folk songs, created by members of folk groups, and cultivated songs that pass into oral tradition has been used by Franz Magnus Boehme, an important pioneer in folk music research, to formulate a universal series of stages in the history of folk song.[6] He believes that "true" folk songs were created only before cultivated music came into existence. Later more sophisticated musicians began to create songs that resemble folk music in their simplicity and their general appeal; these are called *"volkstümliche Lieder"* (popular or folk-like songs), and their appearance coincides with the division of society into cultivated and folk segments. Finally, in the third stage, even the folk have assimilated a good deal of sophisticated civilization. The true folk songs disappear and are entirely replaced by the folk-like songs. This theory is interesting and perhaps contains some truth, especially if applied to German culture. But whether it is indicative of the history of folk music everywhere, particularly outside the West, is something we will never learn, just as a great many other questions basic to the entire field will always remain unanswered.

We know of no essential differences between the way cultivated music is composed and the methods used to create a folk song for the first time. The basic difference appears only after the initial creative act, when the task of the original composer himself is accomplished. A piece of cultivated music, for instance a symphony by Mozart, was performed in about the same way 150 years ago as it is today. True, changes in taste concerning such aspects as tempo (speed) and the size of the orchestra have occurred, but there would be no difficulty in identifying the two performances as interpretations of the same piece of music. The reason for this is that the symphony was learned by musicians then and now from the same written sources, and thus both performances could be equally close to the original composition. Speaking very generally, individual pieces of music in written tradition do not change very greatly in their performance over the years; but pieces of folk music may, owing to the phenomenon of communal re-creation. This term was invented, by Phillips Barry, to counteract the idea of communal creation, which assumes that an entire people create folklore, but it is also supposed to indicate that many anonymous persons share in molding most items of folklore into the shape they have today.[7] If you look for a song like "Lord Randall" in a large printed collection, you are likely to find a number of different versions, all moderately similar, rather than one standard form. None of these versions, or variants, is the original. But all of them are descended from one or a few original versions which have been changed by all the persons who learned them or passed them on to others. Such changes come about for various reasons, including failure of memory and the desire to make changes and improvements. We have, then, a continuous line of changes and additions which sometimes alter the original beyond recognition. Although only one person created the first product, all the people who have learned and retaught it shared in re-creating it in its present form. Communal re-creation, the making of variants, is one of the greatest distinguishing features of folk music as contrasted with cultivated music. Oral tradition itself would not be particularly relevant or interesting if it did not result in this essential quality.

Singers tend to change songs for three reasons. One is forgetfulness. Another is individual creativity, the desire to improve a song, to change it according to one's own personal taste. A third is the tendency for a song to change as it conforms to the style of other songs in its environment; this is especially important when a song is passed from one country, culture, or ethnic group to another. We find that many tunes have variants in numerous European countries. But in each place the tune has taken on some traits of the local folk music style. If a Czech song is learned by Germans, it will in time begin to sound like a German song. All of this applies separately to melody and words; the two components may stay together or change independently.

We must add to this discussion the assertion that the

cultures of the world differ greatly in the degree to which they will allow a piece of music to change without losing its identity, and that there are some oral traditions in which the degree of change in a song is minute and, for practical purposes, absent.

The broad field of folk music, particularly folk music of the Western world, has generally been thought of in terms of two main subdivisions: folk music proper and tribal music. Folk music exists in certain segments of those cultures that have reading and writing, whereas tribal music belongs to the so-called nonliterate peoples. As a whole, however, tribal music is no more "primitive" or more simple than folk music; indeed, it is often much more complex and highly developed. The difference between folk and tribal music is largely a reflection of the differences between literate and nonliterate cultures. But, in one respect, we can also distinguish these two kinds of music by their styles, by the way they sound. In literate societies, folk music is always in close contact with art music and popular music. There is always an interchange of musical materials and influence, and the folk music of a country has many of the characteristics of the cultivated music of that country. Tribal music, on the other hand, is less closely related to urban culture or to any corpus of cultivated music.

In addition to cultivated, folk, and tribal music, a third intermediate category is so-called popular music, which one finds in juke-boxes, on popular radio programs, and in sheet music. It is usually created by professionals, performed by professionals, and learned from the printed page; in this sense, it is like cultivated music. But listeners often learn popular songs without having seen the written score. Occasionally a popular song, such as "Oh! Susanna" or "Camptown Races" by Stephen Foster, passes into oral tradition and remains there even after it is no longer much performed professionally.

Today, in the rapidly changing cultures of the world, it is becoming increasingly difficult to make simple, clear distinctions between oral and written tradition, or among folk, cultivated, and popular music. Songs that used to travel in oral tradition now live, much more than in the nineteenth century, in the written tradition. Conversely, other kinds of music, from that of the concert stage to those of the dance hall and Deejay show, partake of oral as well as written traditions. And the styles of folk and popular musics have begun to merge, and to lose their distinctiveness, particularly through the popularization of country and western music and the creation of folk rock. The conceptual differences between folk music and other musics have receded in the past few decades, especially since the rise of the mass media. In modern technological societies, the trichotomy between folk, popular, and art music easily becomes somewhat blurred.

Outside Western civilization, in cultures such as those of India, China, and the Middle East, the Western tripartite model often does not apply, and different concepts and categories for music prevail. In Iran, for example, oral tradition dominates folk and art music, but not popular music; all types of music are performed by professionals, and the music of the villages is also dominated by specialists who are much narrower in their pursuits than the practitioners of art music.

While scholars have an idea that there is folk music, and what its main characteristics are, today they are less inclined to define it dogmatically. In this respect, we are returning to modes of thinking typical of the nineteenth century, when scholars and professional artists were first discovering folk music and folklore.

III

THE USES AND STYLES
OF FOLK MUSIC

One often cited feature of folk music is its importance in daily life. In folk and tribal cultures, music often has a specific use or is associated with a particular activity.[1] Scholars have frequently assumed that, because folk music is integrated with the active phases of life, it occupies a more prominent place in the community than does the music of Western urban civilization. Today the situation does not seem so simple. Although the concept "art for art's sake" is important in Western civilization, much Western urban music has a specific use—for dancing, religious observance, marching, accompaniment to a drama, or for television programs and commercials, for the radio, and for movies. And music in folk cultures is often produced for sheer enjoyment and entertainment. Therefore, although one major distinguishing feature of most folk music is indeed its use to accompany other life activities, the many exceptions to this rule must be kept in mind.

The most important use of tribal music is religious, including ceremonial music (corresponding roughly to our church services) as well as songs of magical significance or value as charms. Most war songs of tribal peoples are not rallying or marching songs but are designed to solicit supernatural support in war. Many love songs are not personal; they usually do not address the loved one; they are not lyrical, but seek supernatural aid in love. Gambling songs often ask divine guidance; and many dance songs also have religious significance, since dancing is the primary religious activity in many nonliterate cultures. This close relationship between music and religion in the world's simplest cultures stimulated the musicologist Siegfried Nadel to formulate a theory that music must have begun as a special means for man to communicate with the supernatural.[2]

Work songs are found in many tribal cultures, but not in the simplest of all. The theory of Karl Bücher that music must have begun with the recognition that rhythmic work, accompanied by singing, is especially efficient, is probably not justified.[3] The world's simplest cultures, now hardly extant, those whose technology is presumably closest to that of early man, do not have rhythmic group work songs, and perhaps this is one indication of their simplicity. Those tribal cultures that are nearest to urban civilization, such as the Pueblo Indians and many African societies, have work songs, as do many folk cultures.

The amount of music without a specific use other than entertainment tends to increase as we move from simple to complex tribal cultures. In Equatorial Africa, for example, xylophone playing for the enjoyment of customers at village markets is a general practice. In folk cultures, the amount of music for entertainment is even greater.

An important use for folk music, but one that is rare in tribal music, is the accompaniment to narration. Songs that tell stories are common in folklore throughout Europe and America, and these have aroused a very lively interest among scholars. Narrative songs are often not of folk origin; in many cases they were composed by sophisticated urbanites and trickled down into folk tradition, where they became rooted and acquired the essentials of folk songs. The two important types of narrative song are ballads, which are relatively short, have a strophic form (divided into stanzas), and concentrate on a single event and its background; and epics, which are long, describe a series of events centering around a hero, and usually treat the individual line as the most important structural unit.

Many ballads and epics are based on historical events, and in some cases their function in the culture could be considered archival. But most members of folk cultures consider them primarily as entertainment.

Other types of folk music with specific uses are dance songs, songs connected with special occupations, work songs, lyrical and love songs, religious songs, and children's music. Frequently of city origin, hymns have become true folk songs in some areas, but elsewhere the members of folk cultures do not participate in religious folk music but sing only the printed hymns of the urban tradition. Related to hymns are calendric songs for special times of the year—such familiar types as Christmas carols—and songs for specific times of the life cycle—birth, puberty, marriage, or death.

In folk cultures most members actively participate in music; but in Western civilization, music is often a fairly specialized activity, dominated by a handful of composers and a few performers (usually professionals), and specialized listeners (concert-goers and record-buyers). In folk and tribal cultures there are fewer professional musicians and less specialization. Some individuals do concentrate on music— for example, the shamans or priests in American Indian tribes, who have the performance of music as a prerogative or duty. But in at least some cultures, composition is practiced by large segments of the population, and members of a tribe or folk group participate equally in most of the music. All the people know most of the songs and are able to sing them, even though certain individuals in every group are recognized as superior performers.

Professional status for musicians is encountered less frequently in folk and tribal cultures, and few persons make their living by performing or composing. Musicians may be rewarded in small ways by gifts or money, but they earn their livelihood as their fellows, by hunting or herding, through agriculture or a craft. The most noteworthy exceptions are found in sub-Saharan Africa, where the culture and music are very complex, with elaborate courts that sometimes include full-time musicians, rivaling those of the oriental high cultures. Whenever the chieftains of the Watusi in East Africa emerge in public, they must be accompanied by musicians playing drums of different sizes. The Chopi of South Africa have professional composers and choreographers.[4] In Europe, the singers of heroic epics in Yugoslavia, Albania, and Bulgaria live from their earnings, traveling from town to town as singers in cafés and other gathering places.

But most of these professionals lack the rigid, formal training that marks the musician in an urban culture. Tribal and folk groups also generally lack the elaborate systems of music theory and terminology for musical phenomena that make the musician and musical activity in our culture somewhat esoteric. Many people of the tribe know much of what there is to know about music; and there is no distinction between "classical" music for the specially trained and popular music for the rest. But social and musical stratification of other sorts does exist in many tribal societies.

Unlike tribal music, generally the style of folk music resembles the style of cultivated music of the same area. In America, most folk music shares characteristics with an art music style: the Anglo-American tradition has elements of British cultivated music, Hispanic-American music exhibits similarities with classical music of Spain or Portugal. The notable exception in the United States is the American Indian, whose music developed outside the sphere of any cultivated musical tradition. With this exception, most American and European folk music fits into the tonal patterns of Western cultivated music (based on the diatonic scale, found by playing the white keys of the piano).

Tribal music, such as that of the American Indians, since it uses no cultivated system as a model, is often more varied than folk music. Tribal music has different systems of pitch, scales, and tonal patterns. Usually it cannot be played on the piano or on any other Western instruments simply because the pitches these instruments can produce do not fit the tribal pitch arrangements. Some intervals are smaller than the half-tone, the smallest in Western music. Other intervals are intermediate in size; for example, a "neutral" third, half-way between a major and a minor third, is found in many places in the world. Matters of pitch, then, constitute one great stylistic difference between folk and tribal music.

Singing predominates in both folk and tribal societies, and the favored vocal quality is often a distinguishing characteristic of a particular group. Varying degrees of vocal tension, nasality, ornamentation, and vibrato in singing styles are preferred. But although many aspects of musical style may change rapidly, the way the human voice is used tends to remain fairly constant. Often, the tone quality of the instruments in a culture seems to resemble the preferred vocal quality. An example is violin playing in India, which sounds very similar to Indian singing but very different from Western violin playing.

Most folk and tribal music is monophonic (strictly melodic), without accompaniment or part-singing, and with only one pitch audible at a time. Some cultures have no polyphony or accompaniment, but all peoples have at least a sizable proportion of their repertory in the monophonic style. It is interesting to find that the use of instruments tends to coincide with polyphony. Furthermore, there seems to be no essential difference between folk and tribal cultures in the extent to which they use polyphony; the influence of cultivated music, therefore, may not have been a very great factor in developing folk polyphony.

The compositions of folk and tribal music tend to be short, simple, and often very concise and concentrated. Length is usually achieved by verbatim repetition, and a great many compositions are strophic; that is, they are fairly short but are intended to be repeated a number of times. Often different words are sung with each repetition of the music. In most Western cultivated compositions we can distinguish themes, which are more important than the rest of the music because of their unique character and because other parts of the composition may be based on them. But, in folk music, we cannot distinguish between themes and non-themes; for all the material seems, at least to the listener outside the tradition, equally thematic and primary. But this does not mean that the traditional music has no basic, germinal motifs which supply a sense of organization; these are certainly present. Indeed, compact and rigorous organization is a special feature of musics in oral tradition.

The process of oral tradition in folk music is feasible only when the musical composition is organized by strong unifying elements making its structure clear, thus aiding memorization. Unity is created in ways also common in cultivated music. There is usually one main element, such as an isorhythmic pattern—a rhythmic formula repeated a number of times, each time with a different melody (Creek Indian "Duck Dance Song," Example 5a, and "Aja Lejber Man," Example 29). Isorhythmic construction, found in many parts of the world, often breaks down near the end of a piece and is replaced by another common phenomenon, the tendency of units to lengthen and become drawn out.

The melodic counterpart of isorhythmic patterning is melodic sequence—repetition of a melodic phrase or line at different pitch levels. Sequences bring strong cohesion to a song without resulting in monotony. "Ach Synku" (Example 31) is made up entirely of a melodic sequence.

Simplicity itself may create unity. If a song is complex and diversified melodically, a simple metric pattern may balance the effect. Complex melodies tend to be accompanied by a single, unchanging meter, often a simple type such as 4/4, 3/4, or 6/8 ("Lady Isabel and the Elf-Knight," Example 6). On the other hand, a complex metric construction, as in the Rumanian Christmas Carol (Example 1) which uses three kinds of meter (3/8, 2/4, 5/8) within a short space of time, may be accompanied by a simple melody (also in Example 1, which uses only three pitches).

1

Rumanian Christmas Carol

From Béla Bartók, *Rumanian Christmas Carols* (London: Boosey and Hawkes, n.d.), p. 2.

A melodic contour—the term used for indicating the general movement of pitch, its ascent, descent, and over-all pattern—can sometimes be used as a unifying element: the songs of the Plains Indians often consist of two sections that have the same sharply descending, cascading contour, but differ in other respects such as in the Arapaho "Thunderbird Song" (Example 2).

The melodic contour often is a characteristic of each area or ethnic group. Some styles have undulating contours, others jagged, some descending, others arc-shaped. Contours

2
Arapaho Indian THUNDERBIRD SONG

Transcribed by B. Nettl, recorded by Zdenek Salzmann, 1948.

that ascend only are rare, possibly because of the difficulty of producing a rising melodic line with the human voice, for when a singer is exhaling, he finds descent much easier.

The relationship among the sections of a composition is often important in establishing unity and variety. We can classify the forms of folk music in various ways, but one simple method is to indicate the presence or absence of symmetry. Symmetrical forms are quite common, but certainly not in the majority. One example is a type consisting of three parts, the first and last being identical, as ABA. Another, common in several styles of European folk music, is ABBA. The song, "Okolo Třeboně," a Czech folk song collected in Detroit (Example 3), even preserves symmetry within the subsections, as the letter-scheme ABA C ABA applies.

3

OKOLO TŘEBONĚ
Czech Song

Around Třebon, around Třebon,
Horses are grazing on the lord's field.
Give the horses, I'm telling you,
Give the horses oats.
When they have had their fill
They will carry me home.

From Bruno Nettl and Ivo Moravcik, "Czech and Slovak Songs Collected in Detroit," *Midwest Folklore* 6 (1956): pp. 42-43.

   Asymmetric forms may be more interesting. They can be heard most easily in pieces that can be divided into two main parts, one of which outweighs the other in length, range, or otherwise. In some songs, the first part is short, and the same material is elaborated in the second part. Some Plains Indian songs use this arrangement, probably because the meaningful words appear only in the second part (Arapaho "Thunderbird Song," Example 2). The opposite arrangement, a condensing process, is found in another Rumanian Christmas Carol, where the total form is $AB^1B^2AB^2$ (Example 4). The first part, AB^1B^2, is condensed to AB^2 by the elimination of B^1.

   General simplicity correlates with simplicity in form. The form type found in the simplest styles consists entirely of the repetition, with some variation, of a single short bit of music. And although a long piece is usually nothing but the manifold repetition of a short one, variations are often introduced with the effect of lessening the monotony.

4

Rumanian Christmas Carol

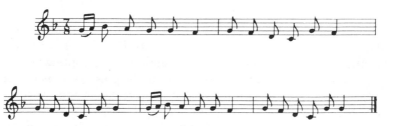

From Béla Bartók, *Rumanian Christmas Carols* (London: Boosey and Hawkes, n.d.), p. 2.

5

Two Creek Indian DUCK DANCE SONGS

From F. G. Speck, *Ceremonial Dances of the Creek and
Yuchi* (Philadelphia: University of Pennsylvania
Museum, 1911), pp. 169-170.

The melodic aspects of folk music are interesting and
distinctive, although perhaps in past studies they have been
emphasized disproportionately. A scale is an enumeration of
the pitches used in a particular melody or piece of music and
a statement of the relationship between them. A tone system
is an enumeration of all the pitches used in a whole corpus of
music in a particular style. Scales are usually described by
the number of tones they have; thus a scale with three
pitches is "tritonic." "Tetratonic" scales have four pitches,
"pentatonic" five, "hexatonic" six, and "heptatonic" seven.
The two Creek Indian "Duck Dance Songs" from the northeastern United States illustrate the use of a tetratonic scale,
A, C, D, E (Example 5a), and a pentatonic scale, A, C, D, E,
G (Example 5b). Most examples of folk music do not use as

many pitches as do the compositions of cultivated music. The pentatonic scales—scales with five different pitches plus possibly their octave duplications—are probably the most common in many styles throughout the world. One of the most common varieties, using the pitches D, E, G, A, B, and a high D, is used in the Anglo-American ballad, "Lady Isabel and the Elf-Knight" (Example 6).

6

LADY ISABEL AND THE ELF-KNIGHT
Anglo-American Ballad

From George Korson, ed., *Pennsylvania Songs and Legends* (Philadelphia: University of Pennsylvania Press, 1949), p. 30; collected by S. P. Bayard, 1943.

The pitch distances or intervals among the notes of a scale tell us more about the sound of the music than does the mere number of tones. A song that uses the pentatonic scale A, B, D, E, G will sound completely different from one that uses another pentatonic scale, A, Bb, B, C, D. Usually scales of songs have one or two prominent notes that occur with

greater frequency than the rest: the "tonic," which is usually
the basis of the scale and is likely to be the last note of the
song, and the "dominant," somewhat higher and common in
the middle of a phrase or line. The very simplest kinds of
music have scales with only two or three tones, such as G
and A, or E, G, and A. Not confined to the simplest of the
world's societies, these scales are also used in European folk
music in many children's songs, lullabies, and game songs.
An example of a song with only two pitches, G and B, is a
composition sung by the Modoc Indians of southern Oregon
(Example 7).

7

Modoc Indian Song

From Jody C. Hall and Bruno Nettl, "Musical Style of
the Modoc," *Southwestern Journal of Anthropology,* 11
(1955): 61.

The use of ornamental tones is common in many styles of
folk music. They appear between the more important notes,
taking up no specific amount of time, and their inclusion is
often optional for the performer (Example 8).

The rhythmic patterns of traditional music are often irregular, but nevertheless systematic. Meters can change frequently, as in Example 1, the Rumanian Christmas Carol; or
a song may consist of a pattern which, though repeated
throughout the song, is in itself fairly complex. Meters such
as 5/8, 7/8, 11/8, and 13/8 are found, as well as the simpler
types.

8

Tune for THE LONESOME DOVE
Anglo-American Ballad

The words are not intelligible; the tune is illustrative of
ornamentation in American singing.

Transcribed by B. Nettl, from Library of Congress record 1725A1; Indiana.

The rhythms and metric patterns in folk songs are commonly based on, or at least related to, the rhythm of the
words. This is particularly true if the rhythmic aspects of the
language are very pronounced. The rhythms of a musical
style often reflect the characteristics of the language. In
German, for instance, words often begin with unaccented
syllables, and nouns are preceded by unstressed articles. In
Czech, however, articles do not exist, and all words begin
with stressed syllables. In some songs that have traveled
across the German-Czech frontier we find the same traits:
Czech variants often begin with stressed tones, and lack the
so-called pick-up or up-beat, but German variants more commonly begin on the unaccented beats. We are not sure
whether these musical traits originated along with those of

the language because of an aesthetic preference in the culture, or whether they are simply the result of tunes being set to specific words whose rhythm must be accommodated.[5]

The rhythmic structure of the text of a song seems to have other profound effects on the entire rhythmic structure of a musical style. For example, in most western European poetry the basic unit is the foot, which consists of one stressed syllable and one or two accompanying unstressed ones. We describe a line of poetry by indicating the type and number of feet. The foot arrangement in many of the Anglo-American ballads is iambic: 4, 3, 4, 3. This rather regular alternation of stressed and unstressed syllables produces a fairly regular metric structure in the music. In most eastern European languages, however, metric feet do not exist in the poetry, and the basic unit is the syllable. Rather than having a constant number of feet in a line, most eastern European poetry keeps the number of syllables constant. There are poems with lines of seven, eight, eleven, or more syllables. The musical meter also may change even within the line, but there is more likelihood of a rhythmic unit, equivalent in length to a line of text, to be repeated with each line.

There is sometimes a close relationship between the melodic aspects and the words of a song. The most interesting examples of this come from the so-called tone languages, in which the pitch of each syllable, in relation to its environment, determines the actual meaning of the words. Such languages are common, and widespread; Chinese and many African and American Indian languages have tone systems. Songs in these languages must in some way account for the melodic aspect of the words. Even though the music does not always reflect the exact pattern of the words, it usually does not violate it too flagrantly. The drum and horn signals of many African tribes, as well as the whistle-speech of several nonliterate societies, are based on playing the pitch patterns of actual words. In order to understand this signaling, one must be able to recognize specific words simply from their speech melody.

Most polyphonic music in folk and tribal cultures is performed by more than one singer or instrumentalist; each plays or sings one "voice," and it is possible to describe the styles of polyphony by indicating the relationship among these voices. In many polyphonic styles the musical material in each voice is approximately the same. There may be simultaneous variation of the same music (heterophony), performance of the same music at different times (imitation), as in rounds, or performance of the same music at different pitch levels (parallelism). The distance in pitch between the voices in parallelism has a great influence on the total effect of the music. Folk music from the Ukraine often has intricate polyphony. A polyphonic song, collected in Detroit, is typical of folk song in the Ukraine: it has parallel motion, with occasional oblique and contrary motion among the three voices (Example 9).

9

Ukrainian Polyphonic Song

Transcribed by B. Nettl; collected by Roman Rosdolsky and Ossyp Rosdolsky.

Imitation, in rounds or canons, is found in sub-Saharan Africa, Melanesia, and western Europe. Heterophony is especially common in many Asian styles. But to these three kinds of polyphony, in which the voices are approximately equal in importance, we should add a fourth, counterpoint, in which the voices perform different musical material. Counterpoint is not as common, however, as those types in which the same musical material appears in all voices.

Polyphony in which one voice predominates is also found in three main forms: one voice renders a melody while the other holds a single tone, called a drone (as with bagpipes); one voice performs a melody of some elaboration while the other repeats a short bit many times, called an ostinato; and one voice is accompanied by an instrument which produces a harmonic background (as in folk singing with guitar accompaniment).

It should be remembered that members of different cultures do not necessarily hear polyphony in the same way. We know very little about the way peoples of different societies perceive music, but it is likely that members of different groups will hear the same composition differently. Some may listen to the individual melody lines as they proceed in parallel motion; others may concentrate on the simultaneous sounds as the tones of the several melodies combine. We should never assume that the way a composition sounds to us is the same as it sounds to others.

Most, but not quite all, folk cultures have some musical instruments, and a few have a great wealth of them. Percussive instruments are most common; rattles and drums, notched sticks, bullroarers, and buzzers are distributed almost universally. Melodic instruments are often exceedingly simple. The ancestor of all stringed instruments is the musical bow, shaped simply like a hunting bow; the string is plucked or struck, and changes in pitch are produced by shortening the string. Some Pygmy groups in Africa use pipes which produce only one pitch each; melodies are played by having each player blow his pipe when its pitch is called for. And there are single-keyed xylophones, which evidently preceded the instruments with many keys.

Other instruments may be compounds of the simple ones. Panpipes, for example, are series of simple flutes, each of which produces only one pitch. But these flutes are fastened together; thus melodies can be produced. The xylophone is a compound percussion instrument; and, in a way, instruments with many strings are compound. Many folk instruments are extremely complex and rival those of urban cultures in technical perfection. The harps and horns of Africa, the bagpipes, flutes, fiddles, and dulcimers of Europe, the panpipes and mouth organs of East Asia are examples of this vast world. And although there are only a few basic categories of instruments, their varieties and subtypes throughout the world are innumerable.

The amount of instrumental music tends to correlate roughly with the complexity of the culture and with its technological development. Generally, persons who play instruments are musical specialists or professional musicians in the society.

Instrumental folk music usually differs from song in the essentials of style, being at least partially constructed on the basis of the technical possibilities and limitations of the instrument, and each instrument commands a style of its own. But this fact should not be construed to mean that instrumental music and song do not influence each other. Quite the contrary. Some cultures imitate the sounds of instruments in their vocal music, and many songs are assimilated into the instrumental repertory.

IV

INDIAN MUSIC
OF THE UNITED STATES

When the White man first came to the area that is now the United States, it was inhabited by fewer than one million Indians, who were organized into several hundred tribes of various sizes and languages. What we know about their culture and music five hundred and more years ago comes largely from investigating their life during the last one hundred years, from the diaries and reports of early White travelers and missionaries, and from the historical reconstruction of early conditions. Most scholars are agreed on the role of music in the aboriginal life of the Indians, and enough actual music remains in the Indian repertories today to give a fairly accurate indication of its scope and style before the discovery of America by the Europeans. Thus we are interested in two phases of Indian music: the aboriginal one, before contact between Indians and Whites, and the acculturational one, including those very interesting developments in Indian music that have occurred recently under the impact and influence of Western civilization.

Music was important in the lives of the Indians, much more so than in the lives of sophisticated Westerners. The reason may be the mystical qualities the Indians attributed to music, the relative paucity of material culture, and the importance of dance. In this respect their music closely parallels that of most tribal societies.

In the pre-contact period, music was closely tied to religion. Music dominated all ceremonial life. Indians used music for ceremonial dancing; for worship, with songs corresponding somewhat to our hymns; for war ceremonies, that tried to gain supernatural aid for victory; for healing ceremonies, in which songs were used as magic; for love-charms and for many other functions. Next in importance was music for social purposes: social dancing, songs before and during battle, songs at athletic contests and gambling games, songs that narrated folk tales. And, of course, there were children's songs, lullabies, and, occasionally, work songs. Though each tribe did not find all these uses for music, it did have most of them. Almost all of this Indian music was sung; there was little purely instrumental music.

Just as the cultures of the various tribes and subtribes were different, the music also differed. In some areas music was complex and highly developed and in others it was simple. Each area had a distinct musical style. But in no case can Indian music be considered "primitive" in a historical sense. Uninformed sources sometimes equate the culture of nonliterate societies with those of early man. Probably we can learn a great deal about early man from contemporary nonliterate cultures. But this is not to say that tribal music, including American Indian music, has not changed immeasurably since its beginning, and that it did not undergo processes of change and development like those of cultivated music. Neither is it so simple as to warrant comparison with infantile creations.

We tend to think that the songs of Indians have been passed from singer to singer for many generations. But we rarely think about the way these songs originated, and we certainly don't picture Indians as composers. The songs had to come from somewhere, however, and indeed they were created by Indian composers; but these composers didn't work or think quite like the masters of Western composition. We know pitifully little about the methods and processes of Indian or any other tribal composers, and probably tribal and regional differences are considerable. But there are at least two methods of composition in Indian life, and they correspond roughly to important approaches among Western musicians.

Modern composers in Western civilization generally fall into two main classes. Some consider the creative process directly connected with the supernatural, with themselves merely the specially endowed mouthpiece, and with little direct responsibility for the shape and structure of the music. Others consider composition a craft, related to skilled labor or scientific thinking. The one group believes in inspiration, the other in the mechanical accumulation of techniques. Among the Arapaho Indians of Wyoming and Colorado, I have found two analogous approaches to composition. One is intimately connected with religion; in fact, the composer gets no credit for his work. It is part of the "vision quest"—an important religious practice among the Indians of the Great Plains and in other areas of North America.

Among the Arapaho most men are expected at some time in their lives to have a "vision." The following account of a vision is typical (from an Arapaho Indian named William Shakespeare).[1]

A young man goes out into the wilderness, seeking a vision. He eats and drinks nothing and perhaps tortures himself in other ways. Finally, on the fourth day, the vision arrives. He faints and then sees and hears a voice singing a song in the sky: "Man, look up here; it is I up here in the sky; I am the bird." At this point the visionary sees a large bird flying toward him singing the song. It alights and begins to speak to him, giving him advice about his conduct on his next war party. Then the bird says: "When you return to your people, teach them these four songs which I am going to sing to you." The songs follow, and the bird leaves. The young man returns to his band, meanwhile rehearsing and singing the songs the bird sang to him. When he returns, he sings the songs for his associates, and, indeed, they are new songs.

From the Indian's point of view, the songs were a gift from the supernatural, the visionary's guardian spirit in this case. From our point of view, we might assume that the young man composed the songs himself; yet he did not do so consciously. We know of instances where Indians sought visions unsuccessfully and falsely tried to make up songs, but Indians make a great distinction between these and honest visions. It may be that in the vision the young Indian was struck by some musical (and perhaps poetic) ideas and that he worked these out in detail while "rehearsing" on the way home. It should be mentioned that in some cases, "new" songs mean old melodies with new words. But often new melodies come from visions.

What does this tell us about Arapaho composers? First, there are no specialists in composition, although there may occasionally be persons who are recognized for their excellence. Second, a large proportion of the men, perhaps most, participate in musical composition sometime in their lives. Each does not compose regularly or in great quantity, but many compose a few songs which they believe they have learned in visions.

Whereas this general approach to composition in tribal culture has been well known for years, a more systematic and rational method has only recently come to light. Our example is again from the Arapaho tribe and is concerned specifically with the creation of the songs of the Peyote cult. This religion has come to the Indians of the United States only during the last two centuries; its music is nevertheless purely Indian, evidently without Western influence, but it is distinct in style from other Indian music. My Arapaho informant told me of two principal ways of composing Peyote songs.[2] One is to take various sections of a number of old Peyote songs, join them together and perhaps add some original material, and end with the traditional formula which closes all Peyote songs. This eclectic method makes use of new combinations of material already in existence.

Another way of composing Peyote songs also uses old material. It depends on a great many Peyote songs being constructed in isorhythmic fashion, in which a rhythmic pattern is repeated several times, each time with a different melody. The composer of a new song sometimes takes an old one and adds to each section a bit of material, identical in each case, thus keeping the isorhythmic structure and the over-all form but creating a slightly different and more complex song. While we might think of these songs merely as variants of the old, the Indians evidently think of them as new creations.

A word should be said about improvisation as a method of composing—creating on the spur of the moment during performance. Some persons believe that the word "primitive" implies spontaneous or unorganized creation. They consider the music of tribal cultures basically different from cultivated music because they think it adheres to no structural principles but is a spontaneous outpouring of soul and culture. This generalization we cannot subscribe to, although a certain amount of spontaneity cannot be denied to any music in oral tradition. Some Indian and other tribal music is improvised, but only under a few special conditions. Certain structural principles govern every Indian musical style, and a composition retains its structure throughout many performances despite its never being written down.

Evidence of the integrity and structural stability of most Indian music is given by the degree to which songs are rehearsed, and by the assertion of the Indians themselves that mistakes in singing are not tolerated. Systematic rehearsing of songs is found especially among the Indians of the Northwest Coast, Washington, and British Columbia.[3] Here accuracy in performance is at a premium and mistakes in songs are punished. Elsewhere, also, we hear of individuals practicing songs for specific performances. Since music is

often assumed to have supernatural power, errors in performance obviously cannot be tolerated in certain rituals. Among
the Navaho, for example, music is the main portion of some
healing rituals, which last several days. Theoretically, any
error in the performance invalidates the ceremony and makes
recovery impossible.[4] Of course, if the ritual fails to cure the
patient, the failure can be blamed on errors in performance.
Naturally some errors are unavoidable, and they sometimes
result in permanent changes in the songs; no doubt many are
due to the lack of a permanent written record against which a
performance can be checked. The errors are part of the
process of communal re-creation, which is common to all
music in oral tradition. Such changes, however, are only
occasional and very gradual, and they do not alter the basic
fact that Indian music exists in stable forms and not simply as
a spontaneous torrent of emotion which could hardly be
called art. That this music can be notated (with some
difficulties, to be sure) in the conventional Western system of
notation is evidence favoring this view, and all conversation
with Indian informants on the subject of music points in the
same direction. The Indians that I have known have always
referred to music as "songs," never as "music" or "singing"
in the abstract.

According to George Herzog, Indians rarely speak (or
think) of songs as "beautiful." Rather they tend to consider
them as "good" or "powerful." This attitude reflects the
functional nature of Indian music, that it is rarely, if ever,
music for its own sake, but almost always an essential aid for
other aspects of their culture. Herzog says that "good and
beautiful may merge, and be expressed by the same word.
This is the case with many tribes of the Southwest: the
Pueblo, Navaho, Pima. The term is applied in many cases
where 'good' or 'beautiful' alone would be meaningless;
where undoubtedly the feeling for the ritualistically good
and aesthetically pleasing is one and the same."[5]

What do Indians sing about? Paradoxically, many of the
songs do not have meaningful texts. These songs do not have

words but groups of meaningless nonlexical syllables. Such syllables correspond roughly to the "la la la" found in many Western songs, but they are more complex and varied and, again, are not improvised but form an integral and fixed part of the song. Often they bear a close relationship to the rhythm and other musical features of the song. But many of the songs do have lexical texts, which do not take up the entire stanza. In such songs, the nonlexical syllables point out and emphasize the meaningful words.

A typical song of the Plains Indians begins with a long sequence of nonlexical syllables. The music to which they have been sung is then repeated, slightly altered, with the entire meaningful text and a few nonlexical syllables to fill it out. This may take somewhat less than a minute, and since the song tends to be repeated about four times, the entire rendition is likely to take between two and four minutes. Many of the songs deal with exploits in war, and the heroes sing about their own adventures. The first portion of the song is sung by the entire group or audience; the second part, with the meaningful text, is frequently sung by a single performer, who tells about his exploits in texts like the following: "The Ute Indian, while he was still looking around for me, I swung him around."

Many Indian songs of the Great Plains had their texts changed periodically in order to conform with current events and interests. The song about the Ute Indian (sung by the Arapaho) was changed by Indians who fought in the First World War so as to deal with a German soldier. A similar change must have produced the following text: "The German soldier fled and dragged his blanket behind."[6]

The reader can gain a better idea of the Indian songs from the texts. Some Arapaho war songs mention their flag:

> Soldier, have courage.
> Our flag has become famous.
>
> My relatives, gaze at our flag
> it is waving in the skies.

The Arapaho vision songs are varied:

> The star-child is here.
> It is through him that
> our people are living.

> Almighty, look down on me, have pity on me.
> I am the crow. Watch me.

> Young man, be brave.
> You are going to a dangerous place.
> Your chieftainship will become famous.

> Young man, it is good that you are going to war.

> Birds, up there in the heavens, come down, have
> pity on us.

The following texts are from the Blackfoot Indians of Montana. Their culture is quite similar to that of the Arapaho, and so are the texts and musical structure of their songs.

> Woman, don't worry about me.
> I'm coming back home to eat berries.

This is sung by men going on a war party.

> White Dog [name of a Sioux chief],
> stay away from this tribe.
> You will cry when they scalp you.

The Indians of the Northwest Coast have more elaborate texts with fewer nonlexical syllables than do the Plains Indians. There also is a considerable difference in subject matter and in the way it is presented. Frances Densmore recorded the following Nootka songs:

> Who is my equal or can compare with me?
> I have forty whales on my beach.

> Do not think for a moment that you can defeat us,
> for we have slaves from all other tribes,
> even from the coast tribes to the north.[7]

These songs are part of the Northwest Coast complex of institutionalized boasting and threatening, a part of this highly competitive culture which has been presented to the general reader by Ruth Benedict.[8] The differences between Plains and Northwest Coast texts are reflected in the music. While the Plains songs are sung in a relatively objective manner, all using roughly the same vocal style with little emphasis on the words, the Northwest Coast songs are sung more expressively and boldly. Of course all differences between these musical styles cannot be ascribed simply to general differences in outlook. Example 10, from the Northwest Coast, illustrates this style; the reader should note particularly the alternation between groups of short notes and long, sustained notes.

10

Makah Indian Song

Text translation: "Good-by, my sweetheart."

From Frances Densmore, *Nootka and Quileute Music,* Bulletin 124 of the Bureau of American Ethnology (Washington: Government Printing Office, 1939), p. 177.

The Indians of the Southwest generally use longer and more elaborate song texts, sometimes divided into lines, and more closely resembling Western types of poetry. Herzog gives the following texts from the Pima:

> Dragonfly got drunk
> Clasped hands with gigikukl bird
> Swaying they lurched along,
> Dragonfly untangled the songs [i.e., sang for the first
>   time the songs he dreamt].

> Where is the mountain?
> Yonder far away rises the mirage
> The dust raised by me rolls toward it
> Many people's yelling, between them I am moving.[9]

Many Indian tribes played gambling games—usually by hiding small objects—which were accompanied by songs. The team that was hiding an object sang songs with texts that mocked or ridiculed the opposing team, thus enabling the hiders to keep a poker face and avoid giving away the hiding place. Sometimes they invoked supernatural aid for victory. Herzog quotes the following texts of gambling songs from the Navaho:

> Where is it going to be hidden [six times]
> Big turkey
> His wattle goes up and down.

> The moccasins are laid out in a row [six times].
> It is going to be at the same place as before.[10]

This song refers to a bullet that is hidden inside one of the moccasins laid in a row. The song evidently is sung after the opposing team has made several unsuccessful attempts to find the bullet.

The nonlexical-syllable texts, although they do not communicate anything specific, nevertheless leave an impression of rhythm and form which causes them to be remembered by the Western listener. They sometimes have a quality of rigidity and firmness as well as euphony which makes them an essential part of Indian poetry; and perhaps they correspond to Western poetry more closely than do the meaningful Indian texts. Because of their sensuous quality, they can be enjoyed on an abstract level similar to that of music, as in this example of a Shawnee Peyote song text:

> He ne ne yo yo [five times]
> He ya ne, he yo ea he ya ne [twice]
> Yo ho ho, yo ho ho, he ya na
> He yo wa ne hi ya na, he ne yo we.

The patterns and rhythms of this text correspond rather closely to the patterns of the melody. Most Peyote songs make use of syllables and groups of syllables similar to those in the text above. Certain characteristic nonlexical "words" are found in many songs; among these are "he ya na," "yo wi ci ni," "he yo wi ci na yo."[11] Peyote songs are new to most North American Indians, and their music as well as their syllable sequences differ from those of other Indian songs. Most other Indian songs have their nonlexical syllables restricted to the consonants y, w, h, and n, plus a vowel. Still, there are always patterns that recur and, most interesting of all, the syllables remain the same from one performance to the next. They must be considered essential parts of the poetry in spite of their lack of meaning.

Questions of text lead us to ask whether the music of Indian songs expresses anything of the subject matter, feelings, or emotions in the words. While this is a difficult question to answer because informants do not ordinarily verbalize on the subject, and, indeed, seem to believe it is irrelevant, it can be said that musical representation of a text does not ordinarily take place, and only a few isolated, even questionable, examples can be found. The closest thing to tone-painting yet found is the imitation of bird or animal calls in the songs. Sometimes these calls precede or follow a song, without forming a structural part of the music. But occasionally the animal or bird call is obviously integrated into the song, fitting into the structure of its melody and rhythm, as in a Shawnee song about the turkey, in which the last syllables "tak tak tak," imitate the call of the turkey.[12]

The influence of pitch patterns in language over those in music is relevant at this point. A number of Indian languages of the United States are tone languages. In an excellent study of the Navaho, Herzog indicates that sometimes the pitch movement in the language influences the music while at other times the musical line contravenes the language.[13] Of course it is theoretically possible for the words in a song to be misunderstood because their tone sequence is not paralleled by the music, but this rarely happens because the words are usually understood in their context. Arapaho is also a tone language, with two tones; and I have found among the Arapaho results similar to those of the Navaho.[14]

North American Indian instruments are chiefly of the percussion type: drums, rattles, and notched sticks. There are some flutes, usually end-blown, like whistles and recorders. They are used to perform love songs which may be sung as well as played. There is no special instrumental repertory. Practically all Indian music is strictly monophonic (melodic). There is no part-singing except in a few spots where local developments have taken place. There is no accompaniment except for the percussion, and only one pitch is heard at one time. Most Indian songs use a system of pitches that is not too different from other folk songs in America, but is more restricted than pitches in Western civilization in general. Often the Indian pitches do not coincide with those of Western cultivated music, and thus it is not always possible to reproduce Indian songs on instruments like the piano. Most Indian singing would sound somewhat out-of-tune to unsympathetic Western ears.

Despite the small number of Indians in the United States, the number of different musical styles is large. The Indians of the Plains sing in a tense, harsh, raucous manner, and their melodies cascade down a series of terraces or steps, rarely moving upward. To us their music sounds wild. The stressed tones are accented violently, and on the long notes the singers continue the rhythmic pulsations so that the music never comes to a rest. The melodies have large ranges with the singers beginning high, sometimes in a falsetto voice, and descending to a growling depth. Examples 2 and 12 represent the Plains style.

Some of the tribes of the Southwest, especially the Yumans of southern Arizona and California, have a completely different style. Their songs seem relaxed; they give an impression of tight organization and rationality. This statement, however, should be interpreted not as an objective description but as an impressionistic expression of the subjective reactions of a person of Western culture. The Plains songs are probably no wilder, in a real sense, than those of the Yumans; but we can judiciously use the term to communicate the character of the music. The Yuman songs have small ranges, fairly simple rhythms, and an even flow. The songs of the Southwestern Pueblos are complicated, consisting of several distinct portions, and often they are sung in a low, growling voice.

The songs of the Northwest Coast have considerable rhythmic complexity; the singer may perform rhythmic patterns quite different from those of the drum or rattle accompaniment, something rarely found elsewhere in the United States. The Northwest Coast has a wealth of instruments and some part-singing, an unusual phenomenon among Indians. The desert tribes of Nevada and Utah, on the other hand, have a very simple kind of music. A distinctive feature is the repetition of each phrase so that everything appears twice. (Example 11 is in this style, even though it is from the Dakotas.) In the eastern United States, a characteristic feature is the call-and-response pattern, performed by a leader and a chorus, in the social dance-songs. There are many other regional peculiarities; the picture as a whole evokes amazement at the creative genius of a people so small in number and with so simple a culture.

11

Teton Dakota Indian Moccasin Game Song
(Associated with the Ghost Dance)

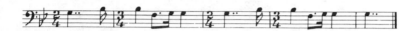

From Frances Densmore, *Teton Sioux Music* (Washington: Government Printing Office, 1918), p. 386.

Just as there were areas in aboriginal North America that were characterized by a certain kind of culture, there were musical areas.[15] And the musical and cultural areas coincided fairly well—again demonstrating the close relationship between music and other activities of Indian life. We find also that in those areas in which the culture was especially complex, such as the Pueblos, the Northwest Coast, and the Gulf of Mexico, there also developed a more complex and varied musical style; and the invention of new stylistic elements, such as part-singing, rounds, and melodies of special length, occurred in these areas of complexity.

The coming of the White man had a considerable effect on the music of the Indians, just as it influenced all aspects of their culture. The Whites brought on the second stage of American Indian music history, the acculturational one. It might be expected that a mixture of styles, partly European and partly Indian, would have developed in Indian music as it occurred in some parts of Africa. The differences, however, between the European and Indian styles were evidently so great that in only a few isolated instances was such a mixture achieved. Indians today participate in two bodies of music, their old heritage and the White man's, but the two are not mixed to any great extent. The English language has made inroads; today, many songs in the old Indian musical styles have English words, such as the Blackfoot song in Example 12: "If you wait for me after the dance is over, I will take you home in my purchased wagon."

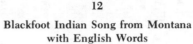

12

**Blackfoot Indian Song from Montana
with English Words**

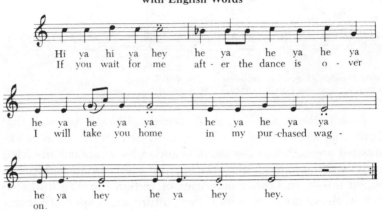

Hi ya hi ya hey   he ya   he ya he ya
If you wait for me   aft - er the dance is   o - ver

he ya he ya ya   he ya he ya ya
I will take you home in my pur-chased wag -

he ya hey   he ya   hey   hey.
on.

Collected and transcribed by B. Nettl, 1952.

The White influence has made itself felt primarily by causing the Indians to unite, to lay down some of their tribal differences and to present a single cultural front to contrast with Western civilization. This was not done systematically and with political purposes. It is partially a result of the rapid and widespread migrations of many Indian tribes under White pressure, and of the forced amalgamation of tribes on special land reserved for Indians. Tribes that previously had had no contact with each other were now thrown together, and cultural interchange became inevitable.

One aspect of this pan-Indianism in music is the spread of two important religious cults through a large part of the United States. These cults made use of songs that penetrated the repertories of the tribes who took up the cults. One of them was the Ghost Dance religion, which arose after 1880 in the Great Basin area of Nevada and California. It was preached by a "prophet," Jack Wilson, who held that, if the Ghost Dance were performed, all dead Indians and buffalo would return to life and the White men would be pushed into the sea. Such ideas appealed especially to the Plains Indians, who were having great difficulties because their native food supply, the buffalo, was being eliminated by the Whites. The religion was preached to them and they accepted it enthusiastically, learning with it the songs and the style that had come from Nevada. These songs were quite different from those of the Plains. The Ghost Dance was thought to be a military menace by the United States Army, and it was outlawed in 1890. But the songs have remained in the repertories of the Plains tribes, and we have at least two styles in each of them, the aboriginal one and the native style of the Great Basin.

Another style was soon to be added to these, that of the Peyote cult songs. The Peyote religion, based on the mildly intoxicating buttons of the Peyote cactus, originated in Mexico and reached the United States early in the eighteenth century. It was introduced to the Plains tribes during the nineteenth and twentieth centuries by way of the Apache, and its songs are related in a general way to the style of Apache music, which is again quite different from that of the Plains. Peyote spread much farther than the Ghost Dance, and it is the most important religious manifestation of the Indians today (Examples 13, 14).

White pressures, then, have tended to cause individual tribal styles to spread over vast territories and to create a variety of musical layers in these tribal repertories, which might otherwise have remained unified. Another aspect of pan-Indianism in music is based on the prevalent idea of the character of Indian music held by the Whites. Whites expect Indian songs to be wild-sounding, cascading, violently accentuated melodies, and indeed, this idea does correspond to the

13
Ute Indian Peyote Song

From David P. McAllester, *Peyote Music* (New York:
Viking Fund, Inc., 1949), Song No. 76.

14
Arapaho Indian Peyote Song

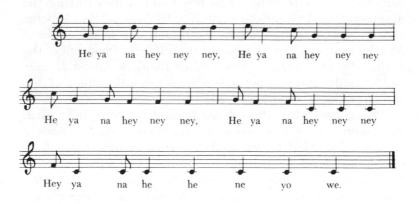

He ya   na hey ney   ney,   He ya   na hey   ney   ney

He   ya   na hey ney   ney,   He ya   na hey   ney   ney

Hey ya   na he   he   ne   yo   we.

Collected and transcribed by B. Nettl, 1952.

Plains and Pueblo styles. Since many Indians are dependent on tourists for a living, many of them have learned this style even though they live elsewhere. Consequently the Plains style has been replacing some native styles in other areas.

Recently, North American Indians have begun taking a greater interest in their own traditional music. The pan-Indian movement, whose songs are basically in the Plains Indian style (usually without words), has come to dominate Indian music. At the same time, professional singing groups have emerged that entertain at social dances and powwows and travel widely, performing on reservations and in cities with large Indian populations. The emergence of White singing groups that competently participate in Indian song should be mentioned, as well as the establishment of several record companies, among them "Canyon," "North American Indian Soundchief," and "Indian House." All have issued large numbers of LP-disks primarily for Indian purchasers. Thus, Indian music is flourishing much more than was the case in the 1950's, although the base for this flowering was already being built twenty years ago.

A concomitant of the pan-Indian movement (which is based substantially on social dances) is the disappearance of many older ceremonies and of certain less flamboyant singing styles that have been replaced by the Plains way of singing. Singers of non-Plains music, such as the Pueblo, the Navaho, and the Eastern Woodlands, have songs in the Plains style. Peyote music, the most prominent type of Indian music in the 1940's and early 1950's, is still important but evidently much less dominant.

Although in some ways we tend to deplore the changes that have come about in Indian music through the influence of Whites, these changes are only natural and inevitable. We must admire the resilience and flexibility of Indian culture, which has fashioned out of the White influence a kind of music which, although different from the older styles, is nevertheless a genuinely Indian contribution and a living force in the folk music of the United States.

V

THE BRITISH TRADITION

The oldest and fullest folk music tradition of the White Americans came from Great Britain. Many of the American songs came from England and Scotland, and upon them was superimposed a native body of folk song, created in America in the British pattern but endowed with the special qualities of American culture and personality.

Ballads are among the most important songs in the Anglo-American tradition. Today they are found primarily in the East and the South, especially in the relatively isolated mountain areas of New England and the Appalachians. Contrary to popular belief, however, the number of ballads current in the North was greater than in the South. A great many English ballads were brought verbatim from the Old World, but since numerous variants were developed here, even more than in England for some songs, British scholars consider the United States fertile ground for their study of ballads.

Many of the ballads brought from England go back to the fifteenth and sixteenth centuries. It is unlikely that all of these were composed by members of folk groups, for the

words as well as the music often show the impact of cultivated song. Nevertheless, these ballads passed into folk tradition even if they did not originate there, and they soon
acquired the characteristics of folklore so that today we think
of them as typifying folk music.

The words and the music of the English ballads are
equally interesting. By definition, a ballad is a narrative song
with from five to twenty or more stanzas. Various kinds of
poetic meter occur; the most common kind, ballad meter, is
an iambic stanza of four lines, alternating lines of four and
three feet. The following stanza from "Sir Hugh" is typical:

> As I walked out one holiday
> Some drops of rain did fall.
> And all the scholars in that school
> Were out a-playing ball.[1]

Many ballads have refrains, some of which have little to do
with the rest of the story, such as the refrain in "The Two
Sisters":

> There lived an old lord in the North country
> [Refrain] Bow down, bow down.
> There lived an old lord in the North country
> [Refrain] Bow down to me.
> There lived an old lord in the North country
> And he had daughters one, two, three.
> [Refrain] I'll be true to my love if my love will be true to
> me.

It is possible that ballads once served as accompaniment to
dancing, as they still do in parts of Scandinavia, particularly
in the Danish Faroe Islands. If so, the refrain of "The Two
Sisters" may be a remnant of that practice, and "bow down"
could be explained as referring to dance.

The stories of the ballads are often tragic, the most famous ones dealing with murder and death; but there are comic and even humorous ones, too. Examples of tragic ballads are "Barbara Allen," the most widespread in America, and "Lord Thomas and Fair Elinor," in which a young man marries a rich girl instead of his sweetheart. He invites his sweetheart to his wedding, but she insults the bride, who kills her, whereupon the groom kills both the bride and himself. In "The Two Sisters," a girl drowns her sister because of jealousy over a suitor. In "Edwin in the Lowlands," a tavern-keeper murders a guest for his money, but the victim turns out to be his prospective son-in-law. In "The Golden Vanity" (Example 15), the cabin boy of a ship sinks an enemy vessel by swimming under it and boring holes in the hull. His captain, who has offered him great rewards in advance, now refuses to let him come aboard again, and the cabin boy drowns. In some versions, however, the cabin boy is allowed to return on board and then marries the captain's daughter despite parental objections. In "The Cruel Ship's Carpenter," also known in America as "Pretty Polly," a man murders his fiancée as they are out for a stroll and puts her in a grave which he has already prepared.

Sometimes the differences between the English and the American versions are considerable and reflect some essential traits of the two cultures. In the British version of "The House Carpenter," a man leaves his fiancée to go to sea, and drowns. His ghost returns years later and persuades the girl, who by now has married a house carpenter, to leave her husband and child and elope with him. At sea, when she begins to weep for her child, the ghost in anger destroys the ship. But in many American versions, the supernatural elements are eliminated: the man simply returns from sea, finds his fiancée married, persuades her to go with him, and their ship sinks from ordinary causes. In "Sir Hugh," the basis of the plot is a medieval superstition dealing with the alleged killing of Gentile children by Jews. A small boy is enticed into the Jew's garden and is murdered by the Jew's daughter.

15

THE GOLDEN VANITY
Anglo-American Ballad

There was a lit - tle ship. It sailed up - on the sea; The name of that ship was the Gol - den Chi - na Tree. As she sailed on the lone, lone - some low, As she sailed up - on the lone - some sea.

Transcribed by B. Nettl, from Library of Congress record 1740A1; Indiana.

It is interesting that this superstition has disappeared in some versions, American and British, because it meant nothing to the singers, and the Jew's daughter became "duke's daughter."

Many British ballads also have happy endings. Lord Bateman, for instance, is rescued from prison by a Turkish lady, who finds him, seven years later and marries him. In "The Gypsy Laddie," a woman leaves her aristocrat husband and elopes with a gypsy. The husband tries to persuade her to return, but she is adamant and presumably finds happiness in her new life. I suppose it is a matter of opinion whether this ballad is comic or tragic, depending on whose side one takes. Examples 16a and 16b illustrate the very widely sung ballad about Lord Bateman, and also show how far apart two related melodies may be.

16

LORD BATEMAN
Anglo-American Ballad

Transcribed by B. Nettl, from Library of Congress record 1724B1; Indiana.

There are also some humorous British ballads. In "The
Wife Wrapped in Wether's Skin," a man who does not want
to beat his shrewish wife finds a solution by putting his
sheepskin on her and beating that. In "The Farmer's Curst

Wife," the wife is fetched by the devil and taken to hell, but she is so difficult to handle that the devil returns her to her husband.

The stories—especially those of the oldest ballads—are told in a unique way. The narrator ordinarily takes no part in them, telling them with no signs of emotion, but remaining objective and detached, and in his singing not differentiating between a stanza that gives routine background and another that contains the dramatic climax. The musical aspects of the performance are equally austere and calm; they do not portray the dramatic and emotional impact of the stories. This might be considered detrimental to the total effect of the ballad, but in fact it seems to improve the performance, for the contrast between the dramatic tension in the plot and the quiet, detached delivery is in itself effective and helps to make the old folk ballads unique artistic phenomena.

The language of the ballads is a peculiar mixture of American colloquial speech and older English literary conventions. Along with such seventeenth-century poetic expressions as "lily-white hand" and "milk-white steed," we find Americanisms like "Stay here you dear little babe and keep your pa company" ("House Carpenter").

The music of the older English ballads is in a style that seems to go back to the Renaissance and even the Middle Ages. It has much in common with the folk music of other areas in Europe. Most of the tunes do not make use of the seven-tone scale, as do those of eighteenth- and nineteenth-century origin, but are restricted to five or six tones. Many of the tunes are modal; that is, they do not fit into the major and minor scales to which we are accustomed, and hence sometimes sound incomplete to our ears. The Mixolydian, Dorian, and natural minor (Aeolian) modes are the most prominent after the major (Ionian). In many of the tunes the melody rises to a peak about the middle and then descends slowly to its original level.

The rhythm of the ballads is largely dependent on that of the words. A line with four iambic feet may be set to a

musical rhythm like the following, with all of the notes
approximately the same length:

Sometimes, however, the second and fourth stressed syllables, which occupy final and semifinal positions in the line,
may have their accompanying notes lengthened as follows:

"Lord Bateman" (Examples 16a and 16b) illustrates this
point. A third common rhythm accommodates songs whose
words are cast in dactylic meters:

Some singers of old English ballads in America use a
highly ornate, embellished style of singing, which is evidently more common among men in the North and predominates among older persons. The ornaments occur mostly on
stressed or long tones, as in "The Lonesome Dove" (Example 8). They consist of short, rhythmically insignificant
tones, and correspond to the "grace notes" of cultivated
music. But they are an essential part of the slow, declamatory
way of singing which America shares with several European
folk music styles and which is called the "parlando-rubato"
style.[2] Resulting in part from the tension on the vocal chords
which some folk singers produce consciously or unconsciously, this parlando-rubato style is definitely a part of the
older ballad style since it occurs in that body of song frequently, but only rarely in newer material, even when both
are sung by the same singer.

In the United States most ballad singing is unaccompanied. The use of instruments is not nearly so common as is
generally supposed, but some accompaniment does exist in
folk cultures. In some regions accompaniment is taken for
granted, in some parts of Kentucky, for example; while in
others, such as in neighboring southern Indiana, it is quite
rare.

Anglo-American folklore has a large repertory of instrumental music for marching and dancing. Its style is closely allied to that of the songs. The most common instruments are the guitar, the banjo, the mandolin, the mouth organ, the fife, and the dulcimer. Fiddles are used for solo playing, and other plucked string instruments, such as the mandolin, are frequently found. Since they are shared with urban culture, most of these instruments are well known. The dulcimer is the only one that has not penetrated cultivated music to any extent. It appears in various forms, but its simplest and most characteristic shape is that of an elongated, thin violin which lies on the player's lap or on a table while its strings are plucked with a quill. There are usually three strings; the lower two provide a drone whose pitch never changes, and the highest string, with frets under it similar to those of a guitar, carries the melody. Like most instruments of folk culture, dulcimers are not standardized, for the instruments behave like other kinds of folklore. Instrument making is governed by oral tradition and communal re-creation, and many variants of each basic type occur. Some dulcimers have string arrangements and shapes quite different from the one described here. Since the dulcimer is also found in northern and western Europe, it may have been brought to America from Scandinavia or Germany. Its revival in America outside the folk tradition is paralleled in European schools and music clubs. Some dulcimer and fiddle tunes are based on vocal tunes and conversely, some instrumental songs were later incorporated into the vocal repertory. The fiddle tune "Soldier's Joy" (Example 17) shows the characteristic use of a drone effect (the repeated open string "D"), common in American and European folk music for stringed instruments.

The drone principle, as in accompaniment on the dulcimer, is quite important in American folk singing. When accompanied at all, most of the ballads are set to a very simple arrangement of chords, often just a single chord, the tonic, predominating almost to the exclusion of any harmonic change. On the dulcimer this is inevitable, but it is also the

17
SOLDIER'S JOY
Fiddle Tune

From Samuel P. Bayard, *Hill Country Tunes* (Philadelphia: American Folklore Society, 1944), No. 21.

practice on the guitar and the banjo. Even on the fiddle, open strings are often played along with the melody, producing an effect similar to that of the drone.

Many of the old English ballads were composed by professional song writers, printed on large sheets called broadsides, and peddled in the streets. These so-called broadside ballads often dealt with current events and news, and many passed into oral tradition. The early ballad scholars declined to include them with what they considered genuine ballads, which presumably had a popular origin. An American scholar, Francis James Child, placed what he judged to be genuine British ballads (excluding broadside material) in a special category and gave each ballad a number.[3] Thus today, although the title for a ballad is not always fixed ("James Harris," "The Deamon Lover," and "The House Carpenter" are all variants of the same ballad), it can always be identified by the number given by Child (243 for "The House Carpenter," 86 for "Barbara Allen," and so on). But the importance of the broadsides, often underrated in the past, is now considered to be greater than that of the popular ballads—in the United States as well as Great Britain.

Well over two hundred broadside ballads of British origin are in circulation in the United States. About half of them deal in various ways with love; many are war ballads; some are about sailors and the sea; and a good many tell of crimes. There are also a number of humorous broadsides, but most describe either tragic events or a hero's success despite obstacles. The attitude of the balladeer is rather conservative and even puritan, and the division of characters into good and bad is simple and standardized.

Most broadsides date from the seventeenth to the nineteenth century and give a good picture of popular taste of a period. Their interest is primarily textual, for the melodies usually were not printed in the original versions. Instead, a melody already popular was often named as the one to which the new words were to be sung. Thus, at the time of origin, there may have been no real unity between words and music.

A few tunes were used for a great many texts, and on the other hand, new tunes were frequently introduced by individual singers if they did not know the melodies originally intended for use.

The British broadsides make up one of the largest single segments in Anglo-American folk song. They have exercised a great deal of influence on native American broadsides, many of which are simply derived from the British ones. The stories of the broadside ballads are not as interesting, and not as well worked out poetically, as those of the Child ballads. The recourse to clichés is greater, the events are more predictable and are usually of little psychological significance. For example, in "The Irish Mail Robber," a youth persists, despite his father's warnings, in drinking, gambling, and maintaining bad women. Convicted of mail robbery, he is imprisoned for nine years. In "The Bold Soldier" a father threatens to kill his daughter because she wants to marry a soldier. The soldier fights her seven brothers and threatens to kill the father, but the father agrees to the marriage and, after more pressure, gives the soldier all his wealth. Many broadsides give accounts of actual happenings, such as crimes and accidents, and thus served to spread news and to keep a record of events.

As many as one-third of the British broadsides are of Irish origin. In English, their style and their subject matter are different from the English and Scottish ballads, and a larger proportion of them are humorous.

Most native American ballads first appeared as broadsides and, typically, deal with real events. Their texts are similar to those of British broadsides. They are presented in a more emotional, less detached manner, for the narrator sometimes takes part and often makes moral and ethical evaluations. In "Jesse James," for example, the refrain of each stanza condemns the hero's murderer:

> But that dirty little coward shot Mr. Howard
> And laid Jesse James in his grave.

The plots of the American and British broadsides are often much more complex than those of the British popular ballads. They have not been in oral tradition long enough to shake off the many secondary characters which have evidently disappeared from the older ballads. The broadside ballads do not always revolve around a single event as do the Child ballads. Some, like those dealing with Jesse James, John Henry, and even Franklin D. Roosevelt and John F. Kennedy, are biographical and narrate several episodes. The order of events varies. Most of the American broadsides emphasize a hero, praise his qualities, and dwell on his deeds, including some that are not of primary importance to the main theme.

The music of the broadside ballads is sometimes in the style of the English ones, but more often it is modern. It is usually based on a seven-tone scale and is in major or minor rather than in one of the other modes that are common in the older material. The rhythm is more varied than in the Child ballads, but it is usually cast in one of the standard eighteenth- or nineteenth-century meters, 3/4, 4/4, or 6/8. While the British material as sung in the Old World has a large proportion of triple meter, there tends to be a change to 4/4 when these songs become established in the American tradition. Irregular musical meters, which we find in older songs, do not often appear in the broadsides. The poetic meters, however, exhibit more variety in the broadsides than in the Child ballads. The melodic contours and the over-all forms are more varied, and instrumental accompaniment is also more common. Indeed, the broadside tunes are constructed in the eighteenth- and nineteenth-century styles of popular music, which include an innate feeling for harmony, so that accompaniment is definitely called for.

Since words and music in the ballads are not wedded to each other, several texts may be matched with a single tune, and one text is often sung to a number of unrelated tunes. If the singer forgets the tune of a song but knows the words, he may substitute another tune with the same rhythm. This is facilitated by the simple and stable patterns of ballad poetry. Sometimes a part of a tune is taken and given new words. This happened with "The Pretty Mohea" (Example 18), originally a British broadside with four lines. The last two lines of the tune were separated and fitted to the text of "On Top of Old Smoky," an American folk song which subsequently became popular in the hillbilly tradition.

18

THE PRETTY MOHEA
Anglo-American Ballad

From James Harrington Cox, *Folk Songs from West Virginia* (New York: National Service Bureau, 1939), p. 32.

The specific relations between the words and the tune of a song are often intriguing. It goes without saying that the music must to some extent parallel the metric, rhythmic, and linear structure of the verbal stanza. The relationship often goes even further, however, to the extent of establishing parallels between the musical form and the content of the words. This should not be construed to mean tone-painting, or the use of musical imagery to represent words and ideas. A version of "The Gypsy Laddie" collected in southern Indiana (Example 19a) shows what may occur in some cases. But other ballads have different kinds of text-music relationships, and we certainly cannot consider this example as representative of general trends, since this entire area of ballad study is still quite unexplored.

19a

THE GYPSY LADDIE
Anglo-American Ballad

Oh, would you for - sake your house and land, and would you for - sake your ba - by, And would you for - sake your own wed -ded lord to go with the gyp - sy Da - vy?

Transcribed by B. Nettl, from Library of Congress record 1750B1; Indiana.

19b

THE GYPSY LADDIE
(Variant Tune)

Transcribed by B. Nettl; collected by Richard M. Dorson in Arkansas.

19c

JUBILEE

(Variant Tune of "The Gypsy Laddie")

Transcribed by B. Nettl, from Electra disk: *Jean Ritchie Sings*.

The musical form of Example 19a could be described by the letter-scheme A¹ A² A²ᴸ. The second and fourth phrases are almost identical, the chief difference being that the fourth phrase is an octave lower than the others. The verbal stanza is also divided into four lines of poetry whose contents can be interpreted in several ways, each with its parallel in the music: (1) the last phrase is the dramatic climax of the stanza, and its music is set off from the rest by being pitched an octave lower than the other lines. (2) The text can be divided into two equal parts, the first dealing with "last night," the second with "tonight." The music is also symmetrical, the second half being a repetition of the first, modified only by the octave transposition. (3) Phrase 1 and 3 are united by describing the place in which "she" sleeps, lines 2 and 4 by indicating with whom. Again, this division is observed in the music, lines 1 and 2 being identical (A¹), and lines 2 and 4 being at least very close (A²). Although this kind of integration of text and music must have been created unconsciously, it may nevertheless have been a factor in the survival of the ballad. While it is not evident in detail to the listener until after a detailed analysis, its effect may be felt subconsciously, and aesthetic factors may direct a song toward this kind of integration. I should point out, however, that the parallels in this example occur only in the first stanza (which is repeated at the end) and that they are not followed through in subsequent stanzas.

Although ballads are the most popular and best-known songs in the Anglo-American tradition, a great many other kinds of songs—some brought from Britain, others native American—live on in American folk culture. Many are associated with various occupations such as sailing, lumberjacking, cowpunching, mining, and farming. "The Jolly Lumberman" (Example 20), a Pennsylvania woodsmen's song is sung to the tune of the well-known shanty, "Canaday-I-O."

Dance songs, play-party songs, and religious folk songs—all are closely related in musical style to the ballads, as are the love songs and the humorous songs which especially typify American folklore. Samuel Bayard believes that most of the songs in the Anglo-American tradition are descended from about fifty-five tunes and thus belong to fifty-five "tune-families."[4] If this is correct, American tradition has benefited enormously from communal re-creation, for the number of variants—some close to the original, some changed almost beyond recognition—of these few original tunes is today almost unlimited and constantly increasing.

The songs of cowboys, sailors, and other occupational groups, are often ballads, and many give accounts of natural disasters and other tragic events. Some have been considerably influenced by early musical comedy and vaudeville. Many miners' songs have been patterned after Negro folk music. Sailors' songs have also been adapted to tunes that originated in many European countries and in the Americas, a consequence not unexpected in a group that has had contact with cultures throughout the world.

The entire history of the United States has been illustrated in folk song. Among the ballads, particularly, but also in the lyrical songs, are many that have historical content. We have songs about wars, giving the exploits of unsung and

20

THE JOLLY LUMBERMAN
Tune: "Canady-I-O"
American Ballad

Come all you jol - ly lum - ber -

men and lis - ten to my song, ____

____ I'll tell you all my sto - ry ____

____ and I won't de - tain you long. ____

____ Con - cern - ing some hus - ky lum - ber -

men who once a - greed to go ____

____ and spend a win - ter re - cent -

ly on Col - ley's Run - i - o. ____

From George Korson, ed., *Pennsylvania Songs and Legends,* p. 343.

unknown individuals as well as accounts of world-famous events, from "Yankee Doodle" to the F.D.R. ballads and including ballads about the trials of Indian fighters. Peace-time history is narrated in songs about the frontier, in songs of the industrial revolution and the labor movement, in the accounts of local incidents and biographies of folk heroes, criminals, gangsters, and benefactors of mankind. Even po-litical subtleties like Jefferson's "Embargo" of 1808 found their way into the folk tradition, as indicated by the following song sung to the tune of "Yankee Doodle":

Attention pay, ye bonny lads, and listen to my Fargo
About a nation deuced thing which people call
     Embargo.

    Chorus: Yankee doodle, keep it up,
              Yankee doodle, dandy,
              We'll soak our hide in home-made rum
              If we can't get French brandy.

In Boston town the other day the people were all
     blustering,
And sailors too as thick as hail away to sea were
     mustering.

I asked the reason of the stir and why they made such
     pother,
But deuced a word they answered me or Jonathan my
     brother.

At last a man with powdered hair come up and said to
     me, Sir,
Why stand you gaping here, you rogue, come list and
     go to sea, Sir.

I've got a vessel at the wharf well loaded with a cargo,
And want a few more hands to help and clear the
     cursed embargo.[5]

The song goes on to tell how the embargo was ignored by the American shipper, and that the narrator finds it unbelievable that "the Embargo's gone to sea, Sir."

The religious folk songs of the United States comprise a large body of music that has been gathered from many different sources: ballads and other folk songs, compositions by itinerant evangelists, patriotic songs, vaudeville and minstrel shows, dance tunes and marches, and old hymn tunes from urban churches. We find not only hymns sung at services but also camp-meeting songs, and religious ballads. A number of Protestant groups in America even today have little musical literacy and transmit their songs entirely through oral tradition. Many of their hymns are variants of tunes current in other fields of musical folklore, like ballads and dance songs.

Folk hymns often were printed in the shape-note system, a method of writing music that assigns four differently shaped notes to different pitches of the scale. Shape notes ("patent" notes or "buckwheat" notes) were introduced in William Smith and William Little's book, *The Easy Instructor: A New Method of Teaching Harmony,* published in 1801 in Philadelphia. In this "new method," a triangular note represented *fa*, a circle *sol*, a square *mi*, and a diamond *la*.

The shape-note system gained almost instantaneous popularity in urban as well as rural areas, and many shape-note hymnals appeared during the nineteenth century throughout the North and the Southeast. These hymnals were novel because they often included compositions by native American composers, rather than being dominated by European works. In 1810, the system was introduced to the Pennsylvania Germans through the publication of *Der leichte Unterricht* ("The Easy Instructor"). The songs in these various hymnals have come to be known as "White spirituals," a term coined by George Pullen Jackson in his *White*

Spirituals in the Southern Uplands (1933). Spirituals are, in most cases, hymn texts set to folk melodies. Perhaps the most famous and long-lived collection of White spirituals was *The Sacred Harp*, by Benjamin Franklin and E. J. King, published in 1844. As late as 1922, the Sacred Harp Publishing Company of Culman, Alabama, was putting out new editions of this classic work. *The Sacred Harp* comprises 609 four-part songs written in the four-shape notation.[6]

By the mid-nineteenth century, the spiritual tradition had migrated to the South, where it became especially strong. From the researches of George Pullen Jackson, we know that the Black spirituals are closely related to, perhaps derived from, the White spirituals of the Southerners of British descent ("We'll Wait Till Jesus Comes," White spiritual, and "Down by the Riverside," Black spiritual, Examples 23a and 23b; "I Want to Die A-Shouting," Example 24). The Blacks have added much to the style of the spirituals and have made them essentially an Afro-American product, but the original material was usually taken from the folk hymns of the Whites.

Among the religious folk songs we must also mention the carols, although the most popular ones (such as "Silent Night" and "Adeste Fideles") should probably be excluded because they have become standardized and associated with school and church. In the areas where the British heritage is still living, there are also some folk carols that are generally unknown in cities, such as "The Seven Joys of Mary," and the apocryphal ballad, "The Cherry Tree Carol." Many of these carols were discovered and championed by John Jacob Niles. Musically they tend to have the same features as the older songs in the Anglo-American tradition: they are modal or pentatonic, having relatively large ranges and sometimes irregular metric patterns.

Humorous songs are common in the American heritage, and they often follow the tradition of tall tales, which are regarded as the outstanding feature of American folk narrative. Some were originally English, as the "Ram of Darby"—

tall as the moon, one of whose locks contains sufficient wool
to make a gown, and whose butcher is drowned in its torrents
of blood. Animal songs are generally popular in American
folklore, with the animals the subjects of human-like exploits,
being subject to praise or censure, and giving advice to
human beings. The tunes are also part of the same stylistic
body as the ballads.

Unique among occupational ballads are the cowboy
songs, many of which are sung partially in a falsetto voice
and with yodeling of a sort. They serve as cattle calls and for
communication over wide spaces. In some of them, the
stanzas are followed by a falsetto refrain, with meaningless
syllables for a text. Others have no strophic structure but
simply an alternation of a falsetto phrase with one sung in a
normal voice.

Especially well documented are the coal miners' songs of
Pennsylvania. They reflect pride in the mining trade and,
frequently, discontentment with the hard life and bad treatment of the miners in the late nineteenth and early twentieth
centuries. Musically, they exhibit many styles, some tunes
being sung to the tunes of British ballads, others to modern
broadside tunes especially composed for them, and still
others to tunes brought from eastern and southern Europe by
men who came to America to work in the mines and who sing
(often in their native language) of their home, the families
they left behind, their hopes and disillusionments in their
new country (Example 29).

The love songs of the Anglo-American tradition are relatively few in number, compared to the other traditions of
western Europe, and they are mostly sad songs of complaint,
of lost love, or of anger at the beloved's infidelity. Some of
their tunes are especially interesting examples of the old
English ballad style ("The Pretty Mohea," Example 18). A
common feature of the texts is repetition at the end of the
first stanza in a closed, cyclic form. Also relatively small in
number are lullabies, with musical material sometimes identical to that of some love songs. Larger in number, and more

lively in tradition, are children's game songs and counting-out rhymes, many of which go back to the play-party songs of Puritan New England, where they served as substitutes for dancing. "When I Was a Young Girl," a play-party song (Example 21), is based on the German tune "O du Lieber Augustin," and shows the influence of other repertories on British song.

Most of the information we have about songs in the Anglo-American tradition comes from studies conducted from 1920 to 1950; in the past twenty years, this field of research has suffered neglect. Rarely have scholars approached the many basic questions which the collected material presents: the identity and growth of the tune family, the role of music in a rural and urban society, the types of change that folk music undergoes when it comes through the mass media before a large urban audience.

Today the folk music derived from the British Isles is having an increasing impact on the musical life of the general public: through festivals and fiddle contests; the emergence of folk singers on the public stage; the developments of folk-derived popular styles such as the music of Paul Simon and Art Garfunkel, Bob Dylan, Joan Baez, Joni Mitchell, Judy Collins; the use of folk songs on television children's programs with participation of such stars as Pete Seeger; and the popularity of country and western music, which is, after all, derived from Anglo-American folk music. Perhaps we may hypothesize that in a period when music experiences great change, as Anglo-American music has during the past twenty years, scholarship wanes, to flourish again when the music is undergoing a period of quiescence.

But several important publications in the Anglo-American tradition should be mentioned. The completion of B. H. Bronson's epic collection and study of the Child ballad tunes, begun in 1959, represents the closing of an important chapter. Alan Lomax and A. L. Lloyd have brought special points of view—those of quantitative anthropology and of Marxist analysis—to this body of music. The works of Archie

21
WHEN I WAS A YOUNG GIRL
Play-Party Song

When I ___ was a young girl, a
young girl, a young girl, when I ___ was a
young girl, a young girl was I. It was
this way and that way, it was
this way and that way; When I ___ was a
young girl, a young girl was I.

From Alton C. Morris, *Folksongs of Florida* (Gaines-ville: University of Florida Press, 1950), p. 204.

Green on miners' songs and of D. K. Wilgus on what was once called hillbilly music are also significant.

Today, folk music in the Anglo-American tradition—indeed American folk music in general—is being treated more like art music by scholars. They recognize that these musics cannot be separated by a sharp line of demarcation but rather that they occupy different points along a continuum, and overlap in many of their characteristics. Thus, the scholar of folk music is more interested in history than was once the case, and he is less prone to deal with the folk singer as one of an anonymous mass, but rather as an artist, specialized though perhaps not professional, who comes from the folk. Here, scholarship and the public taste reflect the same trend.

VI

AFRO-AMERICAN MUSIC

The heritage of today's American Black—his African ancestry, slavery and emancipation, life in the rural South, lynching and Jim Crow, rednecks and the Klan, the migration to northern cities, poverty and ghetto life, Montgomery, Watts, Harlem, two hundred years of racism and ever-present discrimination—has shaped that distinctive body of music called "Afro-American." Since the coming of the first African slaves to Virginia in 1619, the American Black's history has been one of struggle: for survival, for equality, for dignity, for ethnic pride, for civil rights and full participation in a predominantly White culture. The distinctiveness of the Black experience (so different from that of the White European immigrant groups of the nineteenth century) gives the Afro-American a unique perspective. His music, from the spirituals, the blues, ragtime, to jazz, gospel, and soul, reflects his special point of view and his complex heritage.

What is Afro-American music? One simple definition calls it the music produced and performed by Black Americans. Such a notion, however, may be easily carried to illogical

conclusions. It might include, for example, the operas of
Verdi sung by Leontyne Price. Or is Afro-American music, as
the term itself implies, all American music that is derived
substantially from African models? This definition, which
groups a number of genres and styles together only by virtue
of their Africanisms, would include rural Negro folk songs as
well as music of the cities—urban blues, rhythm and blues,
jazz, and soul music. It would also include, however, many
other styles of popular music based on African sources, but
performed mainly by Whites. Some pieces by Black composers of art music would have to be included, while others
lacking African elements would not. A more satisfactory
definiton—one that is more acceptable to today's ethnomusicologists and one which seems to have been adopted by the
Black community—is that Afro-American music is what Black
Americans regard as peculiarly their own. Most of this music
does, indeed, have traces of African origin, but more important, it symbolizes the totality of Black culture.

Is all Afro-American music folk music, or does it, like
other musics of America, have social and musical strata?
Interestingly enough, Blacks themselves do not seem concerned with this question. Rather, they group the rural and
urban blues, various popular styles, and some art songs in a
single concept, which, as a unit, is the musical embodiment
of the Afro-American consciousness. In contrast, the European minorities in America tend to think that music which
symbolizes their ethnicity must be folk music, not art or
popular music. Black Americans are, in this respect, more
like modern American Indians, who also tend not to distinguish various categories of their music. Blacks, like Indians,
feel perhaps that the preservation of their cultural identities,
endangered as both are by Westernization and the homogeni-
zation of American society, demands a unified, monolithic
view of music. Hence, even Indian tribal distinctions have
succumbed to a pan-Indian identity; and the heterogeneous
Black population has chosen a single concept—Afro-American—as its musical symbol.

American Blacks are the descendants of slaves who were brought from regions of West and West-Central Africa. In 1727, there were 75,000 Blacks in the thirteen colonies. By 1800, the number of Blacks in the United States had increased to one million, comprising 19 per cent of the young nation's population. Many slaves first worked on the British, French, Dutch, or Spanish sugar-growing islands of the Caribbean before being brought to the United States. This forced migration of an estimated fifteen million African Blacks to all parts of the New World—from Brazil to the northeastern United States—was one of the largest movements of peoples in modern history. It has had an immeasurable impact on the history of American folk music, for it resulted in the contact of two distinct musical styles: the African tradition of the slaves and the various European traditions of the Americans. After contact, neither remained unchanged.

What musical traditions did slaves carry with them to the New World? This question has no easy answer. The slaves came from societies with varying musical practices—the Ashanti, Kpele, and Ga of modern Ghana, the Hausa and Yoruba of Nigeria, and the Fon and Ewe of Dahomey, for example. And, although the contemporary music in these societies has been studied, little is known about music at the time when the slaves left, generations ago. We can be sure that during the past few hundred years West African music has changed. Thus, our knowledge about the traditions familiar to the slaves is limited to the basic musical features, shared by most West African societies, and which probably have undergone minimal change.

Song is the most characteristic music of West Africa. Songs exist for all occasions: birth, marriage, death, war, work, and worship. Musical instruments are used to accompany singing and are sometimes played alone. Most prominent are drums, rattles, and bells, also horns, plucked string instruments, and xylophones. Much West African singing is performed antiphonally, alternating between a leader and a chorus group, a practice known as "call-and-response." The individual phrases in this antiphony tend to be short, but are often augmented by variations or improvisation. Musical structures are based, usually, on repetition of these short phrases. By Western standards, the melodic patterns are relatively simple. On the other hand, rhythm, perhaps the most distinctive feature of African music, is, by Western standards, extremely complex. Syncopation is common, often resulting in patterns called "hot rhythm," a feature retained in the West Indies as well as in some North American Negro folk styles. Unlike most European folk styles West African music is sometimes polyphonic. The "Baduma Paddlers' Song" from Central Africa (Example 22) shows the characteristic use of call-and-response patterns, short, repeated melodic phrases, and occasional polyphony in the chorus part. These features are present, to varying degrees, in today's Afro-American music.[1]

Early studies of Black music tried to pinpoint the origins of the Afro-American musical style. Scholars focused their efforts on identifying African "survivals" and explaining their presence in the music of the New World Negro. Opinions varied and controversies arose: some asserted that Black American music was purely African material;[2] others argued that it was an integral part of the British traditon.[3] One side maintained that Black music had been borrowed from other cultures, and the other that it sprang, without any outside influences, from the unique historical position of the American Negro. In the 1940's, Melville J. Herskovits and Richard Waterman used a theory of culture change, "syncretism," to demonstrate how European and African forms had, in fact, blended to produce new genres—the Black music of the Americas—bearing features of both parent musics.[4] European and African music, they argued, have many features in common—among them diatonic scales and polyphony—and thus are compatible. When these two musics met, during the slave era, therefore, it was natural for them to mesh, to blend, to "syncretize." A lack of shared features, on the other hand,

22

BADUMA PADDLERS' SONG
(Republic of Congo: Brazzaville)

From Rose Brandel, *The Music of Central Africa* (The
Hague: Martinus Nijhoff, 1961), p. 200.

explains why European and American Indian musics failed
to combine, and remained two separate, distinct systems.

Herskovits and Waterman found that musical survivals, or
"Africanisms," were stronger in areas of the New World
where Blacks predominated numerically. In the West Indies,
particularly in Haiti, Jamaica, and Trinidad, for example,
Shango and Voodoo cult songs which derive directly from
Africa are still sung today. Ironically, these African songs that
persist in the Caribbean may have changed, or even died out
in their original African setting. In the United States the
cotton-plantation system placed Blacks and Whites and their
two musical styles in close association and fewer pure Africanisms can be identified in Black folk songs of the American
South.

The instruments used in Afro-American music also show a
mixing of European and African tradition. From White culture, the Blacks borrowed guitars, harmonicas, fiddles, man-
dolins, and dulcimers. But the Blacks brought some instruments from West Africa, modified them, and made them
genuine members of the American family of folk instruments.
The most famous, of course, is the banjo, originally the West
African *bania,* the Black's favorite instrument for accompanying songs. With significant changes the *bania* penetrated
Anglo-American culture. Another is the "gutbucket," a string
stretched vertically between an obliquely standing stick and
a wash tub turned upside-down. It is evidently derived from
a type of African animal trap in which a skin is suspended
over a hole by a string which breaks when an animal steps on
the skin.

Spirituals are the most characteristic product of nineteenth-century American Black folklore. Probably originating
in the late 1700's, the Negro spiritual first achieved renown
among White audiences with the dramatically successful
United States and European tour of the Fisk Jubilee Singers
in 1870. Today, the label "spiritual" covers a wide range of
religious song-types, including call-and-response chants, Fun-
damentalist Protestant hymns, and the so-called "shout" or

"ring-shout." Although these were once thought to be completely original creations of the slaves, spirituals have now been shown to be closely related to the folk hymns of the southern Whites. George Pullen Jackson (1874–1953) discovered most of these White spirituals published in shapenote hymn books of the early nineteenth century. For example, the Black spiritual, "Down by the Riverside" (Example 23b), is derived from the White spiritual, "We'll Wait Till Jesus Comes" (Example 23a), published in an 1868 upstate New York hymnal, *The Revivalist.* The Black spiritual, "I Want to Die A-Shouting" (Example 24), uses a variant of the tune from the White spiritual, "New Harmony," but takes parts of its text from three other White spirituals: "Amazing Grace," "Jesus My All," and "Am I a Soldier."

23a

WE'LL WAIT TILL JESUS COMES
White Spiritual

23b

DOWN BY THE RIVERSIDE
Black Spiritual

O hal - le - lu jah to the Lamb! Down by the
riv - er, The Lord is on the giv - ing hand,
Down by the riv - er - side. O we'll wait till
Jes - us comes, Down by the riv - er, We'll wait till
Jes - us comes, Down by the riv - er - side.

From George Pullen Jackson, *White and Negro Spiritu-als* (New York: J. J. Augustin, 1943), pp. 192 and 193.

Jackson came to the conclusion that Negro spirituals were simple adaptations of White hymns.[5] To be sure, the melodies of the Black spirituals, on paper, seem to fit the characteristics of Western hymnody. The tunes are definitely in the English folk song tradition or in that of urban hymn composition of the eighteenth and nineteenth centuries. They often have pentatonic scales, the over-all forms usually consist of four phrases of equal length, and the rhythms are not essen-

24

I WANT TO DIE A-SHOUTING
(Version of "Amazing Grace")
Black Spiritual

A - maz - ing grace, how sweet the sound, I

want to die a - shout - ing. I __ want to feel my

sav - ior near When__ soul and bod - y's part - ing.

From George Pullen Jackson, *White and Negro Spirituals*, p. 173.

tially different from rhythms in English folk songs. But when
we hear Negro spirituals sung, we find that many things
occur which are not shown in the printed music. Black
spiritual singers incorporate techniques which mark these
songs as Afro-American. It is not the form and melodies of
the songs themselves, but the way in which they are performed that makes them a distinctive Black expression.

From examining the spirituals, we might conclude that
some Afro-American music results from the superimposition
of African performance traits on music of a basically European style. One possible theory is that traits highly developed in Africa are carried over into American Negro music;
the less developed African musical traits tend to disappear,
giving way to European counterparts. This hypothesis of
"strong" versus "weak" traits remains to be tested systemati-

cally. It does, however, seem to answer several questions about the musical style of the spirituals. Negro spirituals, for example, are more frequently sung polyphonically than are White hymns. This preference for polyphony reflects an African rather than a European aesthetic. Many spirituals are performed in a call-and-response manner. This technique gives individuals the freedom to deviate from patterns as they are sung by the group, to improvise, and to introduce variations. Such improvisation—a highly developed art in Africa—is probably another African survival. Syncopation and other features of rhythmic interest, the use of percussive hand-clapping and foot-stamping, even dancing in the context of a Christian ceremony (in the ring-shouts, for example), can all probably be traced to the African traditions the Blacks brought with them to the New World. These stronger elements have survived in America despite the century-long acculturation of Negroes to Western civilization.

We find these elements also in Black nonreligious songs— ballads, work songs, and blues. Some of these surviving characteristics are encountered even in the recited ditties and counting-out rhymes of Afro-American children. These games often exhibit call-and-response patterns, rhythmic complexity including syncopation, and an undeviating pulse, perhaps related to the typically African "metronome sense." Such "play-party" tunes, once common only in the rural South, are now chanted by children of the northern urban ghettos as well. Some favorites are "Loop de Loo" (Loobie Loo), "Old Lady Sally Wants to Jump-ty Jump," "Shortnin' Bread," "Bluebird Bluebird," and "One Two Three and a Zing Zing Zing."[6]

Black work songs originated with the slaves during the era of the cotton plantation. Similar work songs, deeply rooted in the Afro-American tradition, are still sung by construction crews, railroad men, lumberjacks, fishermen, roustabouts, and prison work gangs in the twentieth century. Themes of the lyrics vary: love, faithful women, faithless women, homesickness and yearning, heroic escapes from prison, protest and ridicule, run-ins with the law, rumor and gossip. Religious themes are also common, especially in prison camp songs. Blacks in Africa, the West Indies, and America share the concept that song can make hard labor light. The singing leader sets the pace for the team's work; the sounds of hammers, saws, the clanking of rail-spikes, all become integral parts of the song's rhythmic accompaniment. Many of the work songs are songs of protest, as are some of the ballads and love songs. On the other hand, the content of many songs is similar to that of White songs. For example, John Henry, the steel-driving hero of the Afro-American ballad, is comparable to such a White ballad character as Jesse James (Example 25).

Much Black music—spirituals, work songs, children's game songs, and gospel songs—had originated in the rural South, where during the nineteenth century a majority of the Negro population was concentrated. At the turn of the century, as industry in the North flourished and the agricultural importance of the South waned, Blacks migrated to northern cities. From 1910 to 1920, the Black population of Harlem doubled and that of Chicago trebled. By the 1930's, Blacks constituted a major work force in New York, Philadelphia, Detroit, and Chicago. In the northern cities, Blacks sought employment opportunities, higher wages, better education for their children, and greater personal freedom and social mobility. At the same time, in the North they encountered racism, which prompted them to live in the segregated, ethnic, folk-like communities of the inner city ghettos.

This period of the first massive migration of Blacks to northern cities saw the rise of the blues as a major Black folk expression. Urban blues derived from several rural southern forms: "field blues" or "field hollers," short unaccompanied calls originally sung by cotton pickers; "rural blues" or "country blues," a solo form often accompanied by guitar; and the spirituals, particularly those such as "Lay This Body Down," which expressed personal emotion and sorrow. "City blues" of the 1920's and 1930's and urban blues after the

25

JOHN HENRY
Afro-American Ballad

When John Hen-ry was a lit-tle ba-by, ___ Sit-ting on his Mam-my's knee; He reached right out and grabbed a piece of steel, Said "It's gon-na cause the death of ___ me, Hey bud-dy." Said "It's gon-na cause the death ___ of ___ me."

From Alton C. Morris, *Folksongs of Florida,* p. 182.

1940's broke away from these rural forms and reflected the new social dilemma of the American Black as he faced the upheaval of urbanization.[7]

Among the traditional American Black folk genres, the blues are unusual, both in their musical structure and in their lyrics. Blues have often been defined as a twelve-bar form comprising three four-bar lines and using three chords—the tonic, the subdominant, and the dominant seventh. This definition is oversimplified; although these structural features may be observed in most blues which have been committed to musical notation, in actual blues performance, variation and flexibility are the norms. A special feature of most blues is the partially flatted third and seventh degrees of the major scale, the so-called "blue notes." Like most Afro-American music, the blues are generally in a duple meter and emphasize syncopation. But the blues differ from the nineteenth-century spirituals in several ways. Unlike the spirituals, which are sung by groups of worshippers, the blues are strictly solo songs. And unlike the spirituals, instrumental accompaniment is an integral part of blues performance. The most typical poetic form is a three-line rhyming verse. Usually the second line is a restatement of the first; the final line comments on the problem or question posed in the first two lines, thus forming an a a b textual pattern. The musical structure, also A A B, parallels that of the text. Blues texts emphasize personal, individual feelings, often feelings of melancholy and despair:

> Well I'm drifting and drifting
>   Just like a ship out on the sea.
> Well I'm drifting and drifting
>   Just like a ship out on the sea.
> Well I aint got nobody
>   In this whole world who cares for me.[8]

Another recurrent theme is that of the city man, down on his luck:

> I asked the pawnshop man
> What was those three balls doing on the wall.
> Hey,
> What was those three balls doing on the wall.
> Well I'll bet you two to one buddy,
> You won't get your stuff out of here at all.[9]

During the 1960's and 1970's, the blues have lost popularity in northern cities, representing to Afro-Americans the resignation and complacency of a past era. The new mood, the aspirations and expectations of today's Blacks are expressed in a new musical genre—"soul." Soul music synthesizes various harmonic, rhythmic, and melodic elements of the blues, jazz, and gospel. It originated in the mid-1950's with the songs of Ray Charles and has since superseded all other Afro-American styles in popularity. More than 90 per cent of the music played on Chicago's WVON, Detroit's WCHB, and New York's WWRL is soul.[10] Soul music—and the total "soul concept," including grits and greens, hog maws and potato pie—celebrates Blackness, is seen as a validation of Black values, and has become a symbol of racial solidarity for the Afro-American community.

The soul ethos has been a natural consequence of several recent political events that have touched the lives of most American Blacks: the civil rights movement of the 1950's and 1960's under the leadership of the late Reverend Dr. Martin Luther King, Jr., the momentous Supreme Court decisions on school integration, the ghetto riots of the early 1960's, the assassinations of Dr. King and of Malcolm X. These events brought the persistent problems of the American Black to the full attention of the White community. During this period, Blacks have sought a cultural revitalization, expressed in today's labels ("Black is beautiful"), political slogans ("Black power"), and group affiliations (Black Muslim). Soul lyrics affirm these upsurgent feelings of Black confidence and strength. While the blues commonly expressed a note of hopelessness (such as Albert King's "I've been down so long, it don't bother me"), soul conveys optimism. James Brown

("Soul Brother Number One") sings "Say it loud, I'm Black,
I'm proud." The theme of "Together we shall overcome," is
echoed throughout soul: "I got it," "We're a winner," "We're
rolling on," "Free at last."

Elements of jazz are one of the major Black contributions
to the twentieth-century American musical scene. The status
of jazz in folklore, however, has caused a great deal of discussion in recent years. Jazz has its origins in folk music: clearly it
is related to folklore, but is contemporary jazz indeed folklore?
Does it behave like folk tradition?[11] Today's jazz is composed
and performed by highly sophisticated, trained musicians, and
is largely an urban phenomenon. It is therefore distinguished
from cultivated music only by its great popularity with the
general public. Some of the most "progressive" jazz is, in fact,
not popular. The usual justification for calling it folklore is that
much jazz is improvised. This practice, however, is not particularly characteristic of folk music, but it was a common
phenomenon during various periods of Western cultivated
music history. In its developmental period in the first decades
of the twentieth century, jazz musicians were untrained or
self-taught. They came from a tradition of folk singers like
Leadbelly (Huddie Ledbetter) and Josh White, blues singers
who, building on their traditional background, composed
songs and created unique, individual styles. These singers,
although members of a folk culture, took on the specialization
and professionalism characteristic of cultivated music. Thus,
they straddle the dividing lines between art, folk, and popular
music, between urban and rural styles.

Early jazz, like Black folk music, has some of the characteristics of African music. The emphasis on rhythm and rhythmic
instruments, the theme-and-variations structure reminiscent
of call-and-response patterns with variations, the improvisation of variants by individuals in the ensemble, all these tie
jazz closely to Africa. And even though today's jazz cannot be
considered folk music—even in the broader sense of the
term—it can be fully understood only in its relationship to the
folk music of the Blacks, both African and American.

VII

HISPANIC-AMERICAN FOLK MUSIC

From Spain, Portugal, and Mexico, from the Caribbean, and from Central and South America, the United States has acquired a striking variety of folk music traditions. Some of these Hispanic traditions, like that of the Southwest, are centuries old; others have only recently been introduced. During the present century, an influx of immigrants from the Hispanic Caribbean and from the Iberian Peninsula has introduced Spanish music to the eastern United States. Miami has a sizable Cuban population. New York City has Puerto Rican, Dominican, and Cuban communities, as well as a Mexican minority. In Newark, New Jersey, and in many New England towns, colonies of Portuguese immigrants preserve their native folk music. In the state of Idaho, the distinctive customs from the Spanish Pyrenees are perpetuated by a Basque colony.[1]

The Spanish folk music tradition in the southwestern United States is more than four hundred years old. In the mid-sixteenth century, Spanish conquistadores explored parts of Texas, New Mexico, Arizona, and Southern California, and penetrated as far north as the present state of Colorado. A century before the British colonized the eastern seaboard, Spanish Jesuits built missions, schools, and libraries in the American Southwest and were teaching Spanish music to the American Indians. The first books containing music printed in the New World were written, not by English colonists, but by the Spanish. Until the eighteenth century, much of the Southwest remained under Spanish rule. Today, the American border separates Southern California, Arizona, New Mexico, and lower Texas from Mexico, but this dividing line is political, not cultural. One-third of New Mexico's present population is of mixed Spanish descent, and until recently Spanish was accepted as an official language by the state. Today it is still spoken in many border towns and rural areas.

While Hispanic music is the oldest nonindigenous music in the United States, it is anything but a dying tradition. The stream of Mexican laborers who, in increasing numbers, migrate to the United States each year continually revitalizes and updates the repertory. It is not surprising that the music of the American Southwest is intimately linked with Mexican music. Numerous Mexican genres, all sung in Spanish, are common in the Southwest: *romance, corrido, décima, verso, cancione, indita, alabado,* and *truvo.* These songs are differentiated, not by their tunes, but by the poetic form of their texts. Most are strophic forms based on the *copla,* a verse comprising four octasyllabic lines in which the second and fourth lines generally rhyme. Sometimes, all four lines rhyme, since assonance rhyme in Spanish is not difficult to achieve (escuchar/hablar; enojado/contado). As in Anglo-American balladry, a two-line refrain (*estribillo*) is often inserted at the end of each verse or between every two verses. A group of closing, "farewell," verses (*despedida*) are often appended to the body of the song text.[2]

In Texas the most popular variety of song is the *corrido,* and in New Mexico the *décima. Corrido* texts are strophic and based on the *copla. Décimas,* as their name implies, have stanzas of ten lines each and a rhyme scheme of a b b a a c c d d a (the "mirror" *décima,* or *décima espinela*). Both *corridos* and *décimas* typically are solo songs without instrumental accompaniment, although in recent years guitars are sometimes added. These two genres are modern descendants of the Spanish *romance,* a narrative ballad form dating back to the fifteenth century, which was transmitted to the New World by the conquistadores. In Mexico, *corridos* and *décimas* flourished in the nineteenth and early twentieth centuries, particularly during the period of the Revolution (1910–30). Printed as broadsides and sold for a few pesos each, they became a type of folk-newspaper, relating current events, sensational crimes, stories about heroic banditos. They spread public opinion, rumor, gossip, scandal, and propaganda. Often, they were satirical and humorous. Because of the topical nature of these ballads, scholars have been able to reconstruct a folk history of Mexico, based on information from their lyrics.

Many *décimas* and *corridos* of the American Southwest were taken over verbatim from the Mexican repertory. But, because the subjects treated in these songs were so timely, Americans were soon tempted to compose original songs for themselves. The first example of a complete *corrido* composed in the United States dates from about 1860. It is "El Corrido de Kiansis," telling a story about the cattle drives from South Texas to Kansas.[3] By the mid-nineteenth century, the composition of *corridos* and *décimas* was a popular practice in the States; most songs surviving in oral tradition today are not more than seventy-five to one hundred years old, and some are quite recent. Contemporary songs often describe everyday situations or bemoan common annoyances, for instance, "Mi Carro Ford," a song about an old Model-T, listing the broken parts of the car—fenders, top, radiator, transmission, battery, and clutch:

1. Tengo mi carro paseado;
   el que no lo ha exprimentado
   no lo puede hacer andar.

Cuando yo tomo el asiento
lo hago correr por el viento,
si es posible, hasta volar.

(It's a banged-up car I'm driving;
One who has not long been striving
Can't begin to make it run,
But when I'm behind the wheel-oh,
Like a bird I make it feel, oh,
Or a shot fired from a gun.)

5. Y allá topé un amigo
que diera su parecer:
—Quíteme este espantajo
lléveselo muy abajo,
donde no lo vuelva a ver.—

(But a friend of mine was passing,
And he gave me this advice:
Take that scarecrow far away,
Hide it from the light of day:
It was never worth the price.)[4]

Three types of *décimas,* the strictest of the poetical forms, are common today in the Southwest. The religious *décima* (*décima a lo divino*) relates stories from the Old Testament. The "didactic" *décima* offers homely advice to the listener, folk wisdom, or morals and proverbs. It can also eulogize a deceased person of the community. The *décima jocosa* is a comic song that uses satire and obscene humor to make its point. Naturally enough, it is the *décima jocosa* that is most frequently printed by the broadside press or by comic periodicals such as *El Vacilón,* published until recently in San Antonio.[5] While there is an abundance of different *décima* texts, most *decimeros* know only one or two melodies, to which they sing all the *décimas* of their repertory. In his monumental anthology of *décimas,* Vicente T. Mendoza, a pioneering scholar in Spanish-American folk song research, gives 572 texts that he collected, but is able to offer only five genuine *décima* tunes.[6]

A pastime which dates from the nineteenth century is the contest between rival poets (*decimeros*). One folk poet challenges another by handing him a written-out quatrain (*planta*), upon which his opponent is then to improvise spontaneously an entire *décima*. Because the form of the *décima* is so rigid, the task at hand is not easy—perhaps analogous to being asked to improvise a sonnet. In the 1800's, this challenge was often issued in the midst of a public gathering, in an attempt to intimidate, and possibly humiliate, the rival poet. Today, the challenge of a *planta* to initiate a *décima* contest may still be issued, but now they are sent through the mail.[7]

The tradition of the liturgical drama, dating back to the mystery and miracle plays of medieval Spain, is preserved today in the Southwest. These religious folk plays, called *autos*, have spoken dialogues and sung portions (*letras*), and are believed to be descendants of the religious plays introduced to the New World by the early Spanish missionaries. In various communities, they are given annually, in others at irregular intervals. Some plays are based on the Old Testament, telling the stories of Adam and Eve, Cain and Abel; others tell New Testament stories. The most popular of the folk dramas is *Los Pastores* ("The Shepherds"), which re-enacts the legend of the Nativity. *Los Pastores* is given during the Christmas season, and although it formerly took several nights to complete the entire performance, today the shortened version lasts only a few hours. Performances of *Los Pastores* vary from town to town, but the standard cast of characters includes Mary, Joseph, Hermito (a hermit), Lizardo, Bato, and Gila (all shepherds), the Devil, and lazy Baritolo. Sometimes additional shepherds, all with elaborate Spanish names—Cosme, Manzano, Aparado, Fileto—appear. The plot focuses on the journey of these shepherds to Bethlehem, and the action is continually interspersed with the singing of *décimas*, *romances*, *letras*, and *villancicos*.[8]

The influence of Hispanic culture is especially strong in the Southwest, but it should be remembered that two other distinctive traditions are also important in this part of the United States: Anglo-American and American Indian. The *indita* ("little Indian woman"), a song type of New Mexico, is a reminder of the influence of American Indian music on Hispanic song. The origin of this form is not known; the word may refer to the adoption of an Indian tune by the Spanish. As this tune was passed on for several generations through oral tradition, the Indian characteristics gradually were forgotten. Today's *indita* sounds very much like the *corrido* or *décima*, but usually the word "indita" occurs in the verse of the songs, or, as in the case of the "Indita Amarante Martinez," in the *estribillo*:

> ¡Ay Indita y ay Primera,
> qué trabajo es tener vida
> si la muerte se apodera!

> (Oh, Primera, Indian maiden,
> To resist our fate is folly,
> When to meet our death we're bidden!)[9]

The voyages of discovery and the explorations that took the Spanish conquistadores to Mexico in the sixteenth century led them, during the same period, to several of the Caribbean islands. Throughout the sixteenth, seventeenth, and eighteenth centuries, Spaniards settled Cuba, Hispanola, Puerto Rico, and many of the smaller islands of the Antilles. As in Mexico, they exploited these islands for their many natural resources; at the same time, they spread their Spanish customs and Spanish music. As we have seen, the folk music the Spanish introduced to Mexico had an immediate effect on the American Southwest, initiating a Hispanic tradition that has continued for over four centuries. The same folk music was brought by Spaniards to the Caribbean islands in the sixteenth century. Now, in the twentieth century, this

Caribbean Hispanic music is making its way to the United States—in a completely transformed style, bearing only slight resemblance to the forms found in Mexico and the Southwest. Caribbean style, sometimes called Afro-Cuban, has resulted from the syncretism of Spanish music with West African forms introduced by Black slaves, who were brought to the islands until the nineteenth century. African and Hispanic musics blended in the Caribbean much in the way that Anglo-American and African forms blended in the United States to form Afro-American music. The predominant African characteristic of Afro-Cuban genres is rhythm, particularly noticeable in types like the rumba and the conga. The melodies, on the other hand, tend to be more influenced by Hispanic music.

Hispanic music from the Caribbean has been brought to the United States by the immigrants who, especially since 1900, have sought work in the urban centers of the Northeast. One of the largest communities is the Puerto Ricans of New York City. While in 1900 only 700 Puerto Ricans were living in New York, by 1940 their numbers had increased to 70,000. Today over one-half million Puerto Ricans are living there, most of them concentrated in Upper Manhattan's East Harlem.

The Puerto Ricans of East Harlem enjoy many kinds of music. Much of it, for instance conga drumming, is performed on the streets and sidewalks during the long hot summer nights. Conga groups include, in addition to the conga drums (played in sets of threes—*conga, tumbador,* and *guinto*), also bongos, timbales, claves, cowbells, and instruments improvised on the spot such as bottles struck with spoons, bits of metal hit with a key, a mailbox drummed with the fingers. The organization of the conga groups is completely informal: passers-by may stop, listen for a while, or join in by clapping, shouting comments, singing, dancing, or playing one of the percussion instruments. Persons of all ages participate. Although the conga drums are generally played by men, women often play the other instruments and join the singing and dancing.[10]

Another common form of street music is children's songs. Some are improvised spontaneously, but others are traditional Puerto Rican game songs. A study comparing the songs of Puerto Rican children in New York with the versions sung in Puerto Rico yields interesting conclusions. Gradual changes come about in the songs; the most recent arrivals sing variants most closely corresponding to those collected in Puerto Rico. In the New York version, references to rural life tend to disappear. English words and American place-names are introduced. The changes in the tunes are insignificant, and a vigorous folk song tradition is evident.[11]

Religious music of Puerto Rico may be heard in Harlem's Latin Pentecostal churches. Each church has an instrumental ensemble, which may include guitars (acoustic and electric), tambourines, drums, maracas, güiros, and an occasional trumpet, trombone, or clarinet. All members of the Pentecostal congregation participate in the singing and handclapping, and they consider music an essential aspect of worship. The *corito* ("little song") is the most popular type of religious song, and congregation members know these simple Spanish songs by heart. *Coritos* are repetitive strophic forms, comprising two phrases of four to eight bars each. Often the second phrase is a repetition of the first. During a typical Sunday service, six to eight *coritos*, as well as a couple of hymns, are sung.[12]

An entirely different Hispanic tradition is found along the southern New England seaboard, where Portuguese colonies extend from Provincetown at the tip of Cape Cod and New Bedford and Fall River, Massachusetts, to Newport, Bristol, Warren, and Providence, Rhode Island.[13] Portuguese first came to America during the great whaling era in the mid-nineteenth century. American fishing vessels, bound for Pacific whaling grounds, made stops to pick up additional crew at the Portuguese Azores in mid-Atlantic and at the Cape Verde Islands off the West African coast. The thriving fishing industry of New England also attracted immigrants from the Portuguese mainland. But new arrivals often quickly left fishing to work in textile mills, cranberry bogs, or wherever they could find jobs. In these diverse occupations, women immigrants were, obviously, as important as men.[14] Since a relaxation of the United States immigration laws in 1965, more than 100,000 additional Portuguese immigrants have settled in New England, swelling the established Portuguese communities. In recent years, many people of Portuguese descent have left traditional colonies and settled in other parts of New England, including the large urban centers such as Boston.

The most prominent folk music preserved by Portuguese-Americans are dance forms such as the *chamarita* and the *carrasquina.* Also popular is the *coladeria,* a fast dance in duple meter, exhibiting many Brazilian influences. These dances, principally of Cape Verdean derivation, are accompanied by bands: vocalists, electric guitar, electric violin, electric (or acoustic) string bass, viola (a twelve-stringed tenor guitar known as the Portuguese "banjo"), drums, maracas, and other percussion instruments, as well as brass, woodwind, and keyboard instruments.

Several varieties of the *fado,* a melancholy Portuguese love song, are also preserved in these New England colonies. The *fado* in Portugal is of disputed origin; but various claims have been made that it was originally a song of Moorish, Brazilian, African, or Spanish derivation.[15] Perhaps there is some truth in all these claims. In New England, the *fado maritimo,* a song of sea life that derives from the islands of San Miguel, Flores, and Fayal in the Azores, is remembered by older fisherman. Songs such as Example 26, sung by a Portuguese fisherman from São Jorge in the Azores, tell of the trials and uncertainty of the sailor's life.

In New Bedford, Massachusetts, and in the communities around Narragansett Bay in Rhode Island, Cape Verdean immigrants and their descendants preserve their own vocal and instrumental dance form, the *morna,* that in some ways resembles the *fado.*[16]

The United States, perhaps more than any other nation in

26

A VIDA DO MARUJO
(The Life of a Sailor)
Azorian Sailor's Song

A sad life is that of a sailor.
What life is more tiresome?
Whose life is poorly compensated
And tormented, tormented. Bom. Bom!

From M.C. Hare, "Portuguese Folk-Songs from Province-town, Cape Cod, Mass.," *Musical Quarterly* 24 (1938):37.

the world, can boast a diversity of Hispanic musical traditions—from the Spanish-American culture of the Southwest, a tradition that goes back several centuries before
American domination of that region, to the recent Caribbean
music of the eastern seaboard. Ethnic enclaves such as the
Portuguese complete the picture. All these groups have contributed to the richness that is American folk music, and
provide one more instance in which the student interested in
the music of other lands can seek information within his own
American culture.

VIII

EUROPEAN FOLK MUSIC
IN RURAL AMERICA

Many other groups of immigrants have had a profound influence on the folk music culture of the United States. The picture has been diversified by the addition of new styles and by the adaptation of other aesthetic principles to British-American folk music. Most of the European immigrants, especially those who arrived during the last eighty or ninety years, settled in the cities. Some groups did settle in rural areas, particularly those from western and northern Europe—the Germans, Swedes, Norwegians, Irish, and French. Often these enclaves had little contact either with the English-speaking Anglo-Americans or with their mother country. But they tried, in their isolated communities, to maintain their European culture. Many of these enclaves are extremely conservative, still preserving customs that have been discarded as obsolete or old-fashioned in Europe. Much music that has died out in Europe under the pressures of modernization and Westernization is still carried on in oral tradition here in the United States.

Many of these conservative groups are religiously based; the oldest European folk music preserved in America is, in most cases, religious music. The Old Order Amish, for example, live in virtual musical isolation, practicing ways of singing that are totally different from those of other groups in their vicinity.[1] This religious group is related to the Mennonites, who came to America in the early eighteenth century from southern Germany and Switzerland. Today, they live in Pennsylvania, Ohio, Indiana, Illinois, Iowa, and Maryland. They farm and, for religious reasons, live a life of considerable austerity, without education, entertainment, or mechanical appliances. Although they can speak English, the Amish language that they often use is a mixture of Pennsylvania German and Swiss German.

Their only songs are hymns with tunes solely in oral tradition. The Amish sing two types of hymns, an old style related to medieval German song and a new style similar to that of hymns sung by other Pennsylvania German groups. The old hymns, as well as sermons and other parts of the church service, are rendered in standard literary German, a language which most Amish neither speak nor understand. This liturgical use of German may be compared with the use of Latin in the Roman Catholic Church. The Amish use hymnals that contain the texts of the songs, but have no musical notation. The oldest and most widely used is the *Ausbund,* first published in Germany three hundred years ago.

The musical style of the old hymns is extremely slow, melismatic, and rhythmically complex. Each word of the text takes up many notes, and it is not possible to discern a regular meter in the music. These hymns are always monophonic, for as a token of humility no part-singing or instrumental accompaniment is allowed. At first hearing, it is hard to believe that they are the product of a Western European group. Indeed, there seems to be no trace of such a style in present-day Germany or Switzerland, nor is it reasonable to believe that the Amish learned it in America, or even in

Russia, where they spent some time on the way to the United States.

The Amish style is a peculiarly American phenomenon, a marginal survival that seems to have disappeared in its original home, but which still exists on the fringes of its culture. If the Amish tunes are analyzed, it becomes evident that they are merely slowed down and highly ornamented versions of old German hymn tunes. The embellishments themselves are slow versions of some ornaments characteristic of sixteenth- and seventeenth-century cultivated music. It is likely that the Amish hymn style is a survival of a way of singing hymns in rural southern Germany, a way that has since disappeared in its original home under the pressure of modernization. Example 27 illustrates the melismatic and non-metric singing style in one of the most widely used of the Amish hymns.

The new hymns of the Amish are similar in style to the religious songs of the Pennsylvania Germans, or, as they are popularly called, the "Pennsylvania Dutch." Pennsylvania German culture is a distinctive combination of South German and Anglo-American traditions. In the eighteenth century, one-third of the land in the present state of Pennsylvania was occupied by immigrants from southwestern Germany, Saxony, and Switzerland. In the early settlements, German schools and churches were established; German books and hymnals were published. A unique dialect developed, based on German, but with many American English phonological characteristics.

The hymns of the Pennsylvania Germans, known as "spirituals," are sung in this dialect. They are a completely American phenomenon—German songs infused with the spirit of Methodist revivalism. Pennsylvania German spirituals developed during the "Second Awakening" (1780–1830), a period of vigorous evangelism and religious activity in American history. The "camp meeting" or "bush meeting" typifies the Second Awakening, and it was out of these gatherings that the Pennsylvania German spiritual grew.

27

SO WILL ICH'S ABER HEBEN AN
Amish Hymn

So will ich's a - ber he - ben an Sin - gen in Got - tes Ehr' Dass man sich kehr' auf rech - te Bahn Nach sei - nem Wort und Lehr. Ja nach dem Vor - bild Je - sus Christ

Der für uns dar ist

ge - ben Kein Kö - nig

sei - nes glei - chen ist.

In this way I shall begin,
Singing in God's name,
So that we turn to the right path
According to His word and teaching,
Yes, in the way of Jesus Christ
Who has been given to us.
No king is his equal.

Transcribed by B. Nettl from Library of Congress record
1767A; Indiana.

Camp meetings were dominated not by clergy but by the folk. Hymn books had no place in these outdoor, torch-lit evening assemblies, and the old official sober literary hymns soon gave way to the simpler, more spontaneous folk expressions. Spirituals were learned at the camp meeting, passed on through oral tradition, and remain today a living part of Pennsylvania German culture.[2]

Some spiritual tunes were taken from German folk songs and a few from German hymns. And, like Negro spirituals, many of the Pennsylvania German songs derived their tunes from the White spirituals. The tune of "The Battle Hymn of the Republic," for instance, is used in several Pennsylvania spirituals.

A typical spiritual pattern is the chorus-verse structure,

comprising a repeated chorus alternating with verses, often drawn from a well-known hymn text, as in the following favorite song.

Verse:

> Mei sail iss so hollich,
>   Mei hots so full leeb,
> Noon vinsh ich tsoo singa
>   Den engel ein leed.

> (My soul is full of glory,
>   Inspiring my tongue,
> Could I meet with angels
>   I would sing them a song.)

Chorus:

> Singet Hallelujah!
> Singet Hallelujah!
> Singet Glory, Singet Halle—,
> Singet Hallelujah!

> (Sing ye hallelujah!
> Sing ye hallelujah!
> Sing glory, sing halle—,
> Sing hallelujah!)[3]

The early German spirituals were banned from the official Methodist hymnals, but by the early 1800's, they were published in German folk hymnals called "camp-meeting hymnals" or "revival songsters." In addition to these books (hymnals) and pamphlets (songsters), spirituals were circulated as broadsides. Through these publications, and through the westward migration of the Pennsylvania Germans, this German spiritual tradition spread in the nineteenth century as far as the Dakotas and Kansas.

In addition to the Spanish, British, and German folk music preserved in the United States, the North American continent is also a repository of French culture, particularly in the New England states, the Midwest, and Louisiana. In New Hampshire and Vermont, as well as in southeastern Canada (especially Quebec Province), a French musical tradition several hundred years old is maintained. Just as the United States is a rich source of older English ballads, these parts of Canada and New England are rich in older French songs.

In the Midwest, particularly in Vincennes, Indiana, older persons of French descent can still remember French folk songs.[4] But, although informants are able to sing these songs for the collector, they are not part of the living repertory of this area.

A living French-American tradition is maintained by isolated rural enclaves of Cajuns in southern Louisiana.[5] Cajuns are descendants of the Acadians who in 1755 were forcibly deported to the English Colonies from what is now Nova Scotia—a theme celebrated by Longfellow in *Evangeline.* Some one hundred of these French families made it as far south as Bayon Teche and settled there in the fertile bayou country of Louisiana. Most Cajuns today are still agriculturalists and live in small, self-contained communities. Their seclusion is partly by choice, and partly due to discrimination against them by their neighbors. They speak a patois dialect, based on seventeenth- and eighteenth-century rural French, with idioms borrowed from other groups in Louisiana—Blacks, Anglo-Americans, Spanish-Americans, and American Indians.

Cajun songs resemble present-day French and French-Canadian folk songs, but have been influenced, particularly in their rhythm, by Afro-American and Creole styles. The accordion is the favorite instrument for accompaniment, and string bands are also popular. Song texts are frequently lighthearted descriptions of the incidents of daily life, the trials of love, the ardent lover, the broken heart—rarely religious subjects. French songs are sung at Cajun weddings, still patterned after the typical eighteenth-century French wedding. *Veillées*, neighborhood social gatherings, are other occasions for eating, chatting, and singing the old songs. Around Christmas and Easter time, Cajun children sing *chansons de quete* ("collect songs") as they go from door to door, collecting pennies, eggs, or bits of food.[6]

The northern Midwest—Minnesota, Michigan, and Wisconsin—is the center for Scandinavian folk music in the United States. In the early nineteenth century, thousands of Norwegians, Swedes, and Finns came to America. The tide of emigration from Scandinavia became intense as the century progressed. Over three-quarters of a million Norwegians came in the nineteenth century (equal to the total population of Norway in 1800), giving rise in Norway to a body of emigrant songs and ballads about the lure of America.[7] Many Scandinavians were caught up in the American westward movement and some participated in the California gold rush of the 1840's and 1850's. Today, Scandinavians in Minnesota preserve their traditional folk songs and many folk dances (*slått*, Norwegian dances, include the *halling, springar, gangar*, and *vosserull*). They also play the typical Norwegian folk instrument, the Hardanger fiddle, first popularized in the United States by the famous nineteenth-century Norwegian violinist, Ole Bull.[8] The Hardanger fiddle is modeled after the European violin, has four main strings and four to five sympathetic strings that are not bowed directly but vibrate when the main strings are played.

In general, it appears that the various ethnic groups in rural America all brought a sizable portion of their Old World traditions with them, and that they practice these with considerable vigor. Nevertheless, these traditions are diminishing, giving way to songs in English; and gradually the principle of oral tradition is being abandoned.

In some cases, European songs have merged with, or

become incorporated in, the Anglo-American tradition. The German song, "Du du, liegst mir im Herzen," has become a part of the general American repertory, as have the French "Alouette" and "Frère Jacques" ("Are you sleeping"). Light, short children's songs or lyrical songs lend themselves easily to this interlingual exchange; ballads, because of their verbal complexity, usually do not, although isolated examples such as "Stenka Razin" do appear.

Some melodies have passed from one ethnic group to another. The tune of a Pennsylvania German song about a house spirit, "Marjets wann ich uffschteh," is the same as the children's song, "Go tell Aunt Nancy the old grey goose is dead."[9] There is a trend toward exchanging folk songs, toward acceptance of English songs by ethnic groups, and toward penetration of the British tradition by a few songs in foreign languages and styles.

Folk styles brought to America by non-British immigrants have undergone at least three kinds of transformations. In some repertories the basic stylistic elements alone survived and were imposed on a part of the British tradition (as in much Afro-American music). In other cases, European repertories were brought over that, in America, live side by side with British songs. Here at least part of the repertory is similar to a living Old World style. In the marginal survivals, styles that have disappeared in Europe have vestiges here.

In the last twenty years the number of European immigrants settling in rural America has declined sharply. Today's immigrants—from Japan, Southeast Asia, and India as frequently as from Europe—have often been urban professionals with closer ties to their colleagues and their institutions of work than to their fellow-immigrants from the same nation. Thus, the flow of folk music from Europe has greatly decreased. Oral and family traditions have declined but the professionalization of folk music and its use as entertainment, rather than as part of ritual, of the life cycle, or of the annual calendar, has burgeoned. The mixture of traditional folk styles with elements of popular music, as the bands do, and the use of such modern instruments as the electric organ have become part of the contemporary scene, in rural as well as urban America.

As among the American Indians and the Afro-Americans, the cultural dynamics of non-English-speaking enclaves exhibits a two-pronged thrust. On the one hand, the integration of groups into the mainstream of American culture is undeniable, and many if not most descendants of nineteenth-century European immigrants have little interest in their traditional culture. For a few, on the other hand, the folk music of the old country—while it perhaps has lost many of its original functions—has become a prime symbol of ethnicity.

IX

FOLK MUSIC IN THE CITY

Folk music was once defined as the music of rural populations, the music of the countryside passed on through oral
tradition, music in a simple unified style. As late as the
1940's, Béla Bartók and George Herzog, modern pioneers in
folk music research, maintained that it was synonymous with
peasant music, an exclusively rural phenomenon. Perhaps
their characterization still holds for eastern Europe. But for
many decades, even centuries, it has not been true of the
West, particularly of the United States. The relatively stable
rural-agrarian society in America is gone, replaced today by a
dynamic urban-industrial order. Today in America, and to a
great extent in Europe as well, few completely isolated rural
populations remain; 75 per cent of our population, according
to the 1970 census, live in urban areas. The remote, un-
spoiled peasant communities have disappeared. Cars, radio,
television, newspapers, and magazines bring city life to the
country dweller. The simple dichotomy between urban and
rural no longer applies to American society.

Since the nineteenth century, internal migration from

rural America and external migration from abroad have
swelled the cities of the United States. Between 1820 and
1950, forty million immigrants arrived, settling in the inner
cores of our large industrial cities. Rapid growth has been
characteristic of American cities; Detroit fifty years ago had
only one-tenth of its present population (two million). In
contrast to most large European cities, which have expanded
slowly and gradually, in the new American cities only small
segments of the population are descended from urban residents of long standing. Most American cities are comprised
of individuals who came from elsewhere to live in the city or
whose parents originated elsewhere, either in the Caribbean,
Asia, the countryside of Europe, or in rural America.

Today's American cities are complex, embracing peoples
of diverse races, ethnic backgrounds, religions, and occupations. We know very little about the creation of a social order
among such different elements and even less about human
psychological adjustment to the continual reorganization that
characterizes today's urban life. We have been baffled by the
city's seemingly insoluble problems: drug addiction, organized crime, poverty, ghetto slums, race riots, lack of housing
and utilities, shortage of vital municipal services.

Folk music in the city mirrors this complexity. It is presented in a multiplicity of situations: music from the old
country maintained by ethnic enclaves, music of societies
and clubs whose purpose is to keep alive the heritage of an
ethnic or cultural minority, hillbilly music, the blues, soul,
songs an old man remembers from his rural childhood, songs
he may no longer sing. Folk music of the city is interesting
because of this complexity, because it is difficult to define,
difficult to pin down, and because it differs from rural folk
music in structure and function.

Although we are a long way from understanding the
complexity of urban folk music, the few scattered, largely
unpublished, studies to date have posed important questions.
Is urban folk music transmitted like other folk music? How
does it reflect the urban culture of which it is a part? What

kind of people participate in the folk music of the city? What happens to songs that are brought from a rural into a city environment? What is the difference between folk music in American cities and those of Europe, Asia, and Latin America? What is the role of music in the interaction of ethnic and racial groups in the city?

One of the earliest of urban music field projects was begun in 1939 in Detroit by faculty and students at Wayne State University.[1] Since that time, investigations have been conducted among the city's Poles, Italians, Ukrainians, Yugoslavians, Estonians, Mexicans, Syrians, Chinese, American Indians, and rural Black and White migrants. Much of the music collected in Detroit was brought in by migrants from the countryside and perpetuated by communities only slightly removed from their rural roots.

The Detroit White English-speaking community from the South has lost much of its Anglo-American folk song tradition. Folk songs are not often passed from parents to children after the family arrives in the city. Their musical life is taken out of oral tradition, removed from the hands of the family, and entrusted to the care of the folk song disk jockey. The southern White immigrants have left the tradition of active participation and have become spectators and listeners in the pattern of modern city entertainment. They know the hillbilly songs well, but they do not sing them or teach them to their children. Instead, these songs are propagated by professional musicians in taverns and on radio and television. When a song is dropped from these outlets of entertainment, it also dies in the minds of the Anglo-American viewers. Popular ballads, broadsides, and lyrical songs seem gradually to disappear from their tradition, except those kept alive by a few professional entertainers.

The other English-speaking group that has recently arrived in the cities of the North, the southern Blacks, seems to have retained only a little more of its rural folk tradition than the southern Whites. Blacks seem to have kept at least a part of their religious folk song tradition—the spirituals—but their

interest in secular folk songs has almost always been transformed into an interest in commercial Black popular songs on
records, performed by professionals who become the focus of
hero worship by both Blacks and Whites. Interest in the folk
blues has been turned into love for the popular blues; the
singing of work songs has been replaced by listening to
old-time jazz. Above all, soul music has captured Black audiences and the "soul ethos" has been called the great folk
myth of the modern Black.

The religious songs of the folk tradition, however, unlike
the secular songs, are conserved in the urban environment
with little or no change. There are several possible reasons.
Some churches frown on the use of recorded material or
radio, so the spirituals must be passed on by oral tradition.
Those Afro-Americans whose family cohesion is strongest are
often the most devout; and, since the family is usually an
important unit in oral tradition, word-of-mouth transmission
favors religious material. On the other hand, many Blacks
prefer soul and other popular music because it solidifies their
urban status and is a field in which they, as a group, enjoy
prestige among Whites. The Blacks in industrial cities are
avid record fans; the number of record stores in Black resi-
dential areas is disproportionately great, even in the poverty-
stricken districts. Blacks seem to have a greater desire to be
urbanized than the southern Whites. The Whites are often
transient, returning periodically to the South; they remain
rural in spirit. Most Blacks in the North have no intention of
returning to the South.

The non-English-speaking groups of the newer American
cities are much more conscious of their folk music heritage
than the native Americans. For these foreign immigrants, folk
music is a way of retaining the cohesion of their ethnic
groups, but it is also a method of impressing and gaining the
respect of others. In a foreign environment, ethnic groups
must work hard to achieve musical continuity. Minorities do
not usually trust the channels of oral tradition to assure the
survival of their songs. Instead, European and Asian ethnic

groups often organize singing societies and clubs, found religious bodies, sponsor professional entertainers, and develop musical specialists. Often groups have semiofficial organizations that try to ensure the preservation of the folk music heritage.[2] Choirs and bands are led by specialists in folk music who, although they participate in the folk tradition, are often trained professionally—have at least a semiprofessional status—and also specialize in teaching folk music. Folk music becomes the concern of intellectual leaders of the ethnic groups. Thus, while folk music of the old country is retained in the life of the ethnic group, it is changed under the pressure of Americanization and urbanization.

Immigrants often use semiofficial musical organizations as one means of adapting to an unfamiliar urban environment. These organizations serve both to integrate and to unify the members of the ethnic group, while segregating them from the larger community. Often the membership of such organizations is heterogeneous, including persons who share a common ethnic identity but who probably had no reason to meet together before coming to the United States. A good example is the some 50,000 recent immigrants from India in New York City. Most Indians have come to the United States during the last twenty years, most are well-educated professional men and women—doctors, nurses, lawyers, and engineers. Most are from the upper castes, classes, and income brackets of Indian society. But they come from all corners of India, speak many mutually unintelligible languages (English and Hindi are used as *lingua franca*), are of various religious sects, have distinctive cultural backgrounds and different musical repertories. These regional differences are certainly important in India but they tend to break down in New York. New York Indians have organized nearly a dozen Hindu temple societies that hold regular services. The singing of *bhajan*s, Hindu devotional songs, is an integral part of service worship. Only a few of these temples comprise members from one particular locale in India. The Sikh temple does have a congregation almost entirely from the Punjab.

Punjabi is spoken and the traditional music of this area of India is used in the Sikh services. Most temples, however, draw together Hindus from various parts of the subcontinent. These groups have pooled their musical repertories. Good singers from the various Indian states sing in their regional languages the *bhajans* they like best, while the others listen. The congregation sings together those songs that are known all over India. Often these are traditional songs that achieved popularity from being used in one or several Indian films. "Jay Jagadiisha Haree" (Example 28), is a *bhajan* familiar to Indians everywhere and is sung at the close of nearly all Hindu services in New York.

Included in New York City's Indian community is a small enclave of East Indians from the West Indies. During the nineteenth-century, indentured laborers from India were brought to work on the sugar cane plantations of Trinidad, Guyana, Surinam, Barbados, and Jamaica. Many of these Indians settled permanently in the Caribbean area and they now constitute a major segment of the population in Trinidad and Guyana. Some Trinidad and Guyanese Indians have recently migrated to New York City, seeking greater employment opportunities and higher wages. These Caribbean Indians have also formed a Hindu temple society which holds a weekly service, called a *puja*. *Puja* includes the singing of *bhajans*, the chanting of Sanskrit prayers (*mantras*), the Sanskrit chanting of the *Havaan* (thanksgiving) ceremony, and the giving of *aartee* (a fire offering) to the deities of the Hindu pantheon. During *aartee,* the *bhajan* "Jay Jagadiisha Haree" is always sung by the entire congregation. The singing is accompanied by familiar North Indian instruments: the harmonium (a small keyboard instrument), the *dholak* (a double-headed drum played with both hands), the *dantal* (a three-foot iron rod, beaten with a piece of metal), and *majeera* (finger cymbals). Trinidadian and Guyanese Indians of all faiths attend this weekly service, thus keeping in touch with fellow countrymen scattered throughout the metropolitan area. To accommodate non-Hindu members, Muslim

28

JAY JAGADIISHA HAREE
Hindu Bhajan

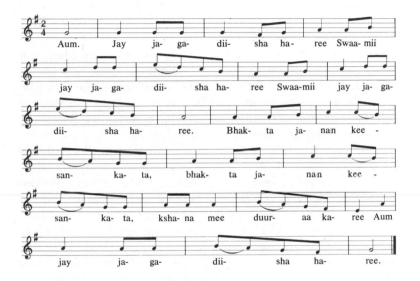

Aum. Jay ja- ga- dii- sha ha- ree Swaa- mii
jay ja- ga- dii- sha ha- ree Swaa-mii jay ja- ga-
dii- sha ha- ree. Bhak- ta ja- nan kee -
san- ka- ta, bhak- ta ja- nan kee -
san- ka- ta, ksha- na mee duur- aa ka- ree Aum
jay ja- ga- dii- sha ha- ree.

Hail lord of the world, Swaami hail lord of the world,
Know the trouble of your devotee, make it go far away.

Collected and transcribed by Helen Myers, New York
City, 1975.

prayers in Urdu (the language of Pakistan and parts of Muslim North India) and Christian prayers in English are included in the service.

The New York City context provides East Indians from the Caribbean (most of whom have never seen India) with an opportunity to meet other immigrants, born and raised in India. The results of these meetings are interesting musically. India-born immigrants, who from time to time attend the Trinidadian service, often claim that the performance of the traditional Indian songs is less than satisfactory. They may point out that the Hindi words of song texts are mispronounced and that the *bhajan*s which are sung are often not "genuine" traditional songs but film songs, even love songs. When India-born Hindus try to lead a *bhajan*, the Trinidadian and Guyanese congregation may not join in the singing and the instrumentalists generally have difficulty following the *tala* (rhythmic pattern).

This congregation of Christians, Muslims, and Hindus—Trinidadian, Guyanese, and Indian nationals—is an apt illustration of the heterogeneous groups that the urban environment engenders. This particular organization is less than ten years old, but as time passes it will be significant to note how various factions within the society influence the development of a new musical repertory, uniquely suited to this unusual group. Cities in America provide the student of folk music with countless such opportunities to study the process of culture contact as it influences musical change.

General participation in folk song, one of the marks of most rural musical cultures, is often weakened in the city. Whereas a large segment of the population may still participate fully, there is a tendency to develop specialists in folk song, individuals who are not professional musicians but who, because of their great knowledge of folk songs and their interest in them, are recognized as guardians of the tradition. Among the Polish residents of Detroit, the largest ethnic group in the area, they are the cooks who cater at weddings and who also perform the musical parts of the marriage ritual.

These cooks evidently know hundreds of songs, wedding songs and other kinds, and they act as consultants in folk song and folklore.

Much folk music of ethnic groups retains its original function. Wedding songs are still performed at weddings, dance songs are used for dancing. A collection of Pittsburgh industrial folk songs includes, besides a number of union songs, some in the native language of the foreign-born workers, sung to eastern and southern European tunes (Example 29). Others are in English and occasionally make use of the tunes current in popular and broadside balladry, such as the following text, which is sung to the tune of the well-known "Crawdad Song."

> Pittsburgh is a great old town, Pittsburgh;
> Pittsburgh is a great old town, Pittsburgh;
> Pittsburgh is a great old town,
> Solid steel from McKeesport down.
> Pittsburgh is a great old town, Pittsburgh.[3]

Other songs remembered by immigrants tell of rural life and have no analogous purpose in the city environment; "Hraly Dudy" and "Ach Synku" (Examples 30 and 31) are Czech songs of agriculture and peasant life as remembered by an immigrant from Czechoslovakia who came to Detroit in 1948. Possibly such songs will be perpetuated through oral tradition in the city setting. But it is more likely that they will be forgotten in a few generations.

Because the rural function of a song is often lost in the city context, the music of folk songs becomes more important to members of the ethnic group. According to some informants, the quality of a tune is a greater factor in the survival of a song in America than are its words. It is also interesting that folk dancing and knowledge of its details are more widespread than singing.

Nevertheless, in many instances, oral tradition does survive. A young Polish informant in Detroit, whose grand-

29
AJA LEJBER MAN
Slovak Industrial Song

A - ja Lej - ber man,   ro - bim k a - ždi den,

vše   se - be   ra - hu - jem   ke - lo   zo - spo - ru - jem,

ko -   lo   zo - spo - ru - jem na -   ti -   dzen.

I'm a labor man,
I work every day.
To myself I always figure
"How much am I saving,
How much am I saving each week?"

From George Korson, ed., *Pennsylvania Songs and Legends*, p. 436.

parents emigrated to this country over sixty years ago, knew in 1958 many songs, all learned from his relatives, and he indicated that this is typical. Indeed, he believed that most of the second- and third-generation Polish-Americans knew more folk songs than do those who had arrived in the United States after World War II. The practice of folk music evidently decreased in Poland in the course of the twentieth century. This fact is of great interest, for it reaffirms the theory of marginal survivals, and shows that the United States is a center for marginal survivals. In this case, Polish folk songs have evidently decreased in number and strength at the center of their distribution, the homeland, probably under the pressure of urbanization, industrialization, and political propaganda. But in the outskirts of Polish culture,

30

HRALY DUDY
Czech Song

Hrá - li du - dy u po - bu - dy, já jsem je sly - še - la.

Dá - va - li mi ko - me - ní - ka já jsem ho ne - chtě - la.

A já rad - ši krej - či - ho, To je ně - co lep - ši - ho.

U - ši - je mi šne - ro - vač - ku ze sa - mý - ho ci - zí - ho.

4. The bagpipes played at the tramp's house,
I listened to them.
They were marrying me to a chimney-sweep;
I didn't want him.
I prefer a tailor.
That is something better.
He will make me a corset
Out of foreign cloth.

From Bruno Nettl and Ivo Moravcik, "Czech and Slovak
Songs Collected in Detroit," *Midwest Folklore* 5 (1955):
40–41.

among the Polish-Americans who left their homeland when
folk music was flourishing, the songs have persisted for a
longer time and have been more durable.

Musical instruments play a larger part in the folk music of
Detroit than of rural areas, probably because of the prepon-
derance of instrumental music in the city. Instruments are
used often, both for solo and accompaniment, and proficiency
on an instrument is demanded of most folk singers. Among

31
ACH SYNKU
Czech Song

Ach syn - ku syn - ku, do - ma - li jsi?

Ach syn - ku, syn - ku, do - ma - li jsi?

Ta - tí - ček se — ptá o - ral - li jsi,

ta - tí - ček se — ptá, o - ral - li jsi.

Oh, son, son, are you at home?
Father is asking, have you plowed?

From Bruno Nettl and Ivo Moravcik, "Czech and Slovak
Songs Collected in Detroit," pp. 40–41.

the Poles in Detroit, songs which must be sung unaccompanied have declined more rapidly than accompanied songs. Instrumental music is often favored over vocal in communities with two or more ethnic groups who do not speak the same language. This is the situation in New York's East Harlem. When Spanish-speaking Puerto Ricans and English-speaking Blacks participate in joint functions, they generally select instrumental music, thus minimizing the language barrier.

Another aspect of most rural folk songs is communal re-creation, the development of variants by creative change on the part of the singers. We are not at all sure whether communal re-creation occurs in urban folk music. The indications are that it is weaker than in the country and that standardization is more general. A partial reason must be the rather frequent use of printed folk song collections, albums, and records. Another is the development of specialists who standardize their versions and develop conscious musical behavior.

What fate may the folk songs of foreign ethnic groups have in the future? It is possible that the songs will share the fate of ethnic groups themselves, some of which have been decreasing in size and strength. We can answer this question from the point of view of individual informants. It appears, for example, that the oldest child in a family of Polish settlers knows more folk songs than the younger children. The extent of ethnic knowledge a Polish informant has seems to correlate with the amount of Polish he speaks. The amount of music known by native members of the ethnic group is smaller than that of their immigrant parents, and recent arrivals are better versed than old-time United States residents. There is no doubt, however, that some types of folk music, especially those associated with functions that remain in practice, such as dancing, survive for several generations. The American city, in contrast with its European counterpart, is a storehouse of European folk music which is kept alive in the enclaves that perpetuate their original rural culture.

The study of music in the city has only recently become an integral part of American folklore and musicological research. Urban ethnomusicology to date has dealt almost exclusively with music of ethnic enclaves in the city. The techniques, theories, and methods developed for the study of rural folk music or the tribal music of simple societies have had to be modified in order to deal with the complexity of interrelationships among the groups that make up an American city. The interaction among the diverse folk musics of the city, the impact of urban problems on music, and the role of music in the complexity of urban life are only now beginning to be explored, and nothing approaching a comprehensive musical ethnography of any individual American city has yet been compiled. Scholars are only beginning to gather information about the new folk genres (such as urban blues and

soul), born in the context of the metropolis. We are finding
that the city is an ideal setting for the study of musical
change. We see ethnic enclaves adapting their rural folk
songs to the urban environment. We see some ethnic repertories dying out while others flourish through the efforts of
revivalists. For the student of folk music, American cities
promise to be exciting areas for future research.

X

STUDYING FOLK MUSIC

The study of folk music in its cultural context is a part of ethnomusicology, a field that combines methods and approaches from several disciplines. The raw material is collected with the techniques of anthropology and classified with the techniques of folklore. It is then set down on paper and analyzed through the methods of musicology, but results of the analysis are usually interpreted in the light of anthropological theory. The scholar who wishes to do a complete job of studying folk music should be familiar with all these fields.

Before 1950, ethnomusicology was known as "comparative musicology." This label reflects the desire of founding fathers of the field—Carl Stumpf, Alexander J. Ellis, Erich M. von Hornbostel—to understand music as a universal, rather than as a strictly Western, phenomenon. Many of the nineteenth-century European scholars sought to discover the ultimate origins of music by investigating songs of so-called "primitive" cultures. Others felt their mission was the study of all "exotic" non-Western music, a subject neglected by the scholars of music history. By the beginning of the twentieth century in both Europe and America, musicologists concerned with comparative studies believed they were working against time. Folk music, even "the folk" themselves, scholars feared, were fast disappearing. Preservation of the world's traditional music for future generations became the prime research objective, and collecting was the urgent task at hand. Archives for the storing of recorded materials were founded, the first of these being the Berlin and Vienna Phonogramm Archives, established around 1900. Several important archives were founded in the United States, including the Archives of American Folksong in the Library of Congress and the Archives of Traditional Music at Indiana University.

Preservation of traditional music as a goal still characterizes some ethnomusicological research, but it is becoming apparent that the task is impossible. The music of all cultures is undergoing constant change; as older bodies of music die out, new ones are born. Today, emphasis in ethnomusicology has shifted from the frantic scramble to record this potentially limitless material, from collecting for collecting's sake, to understanding man through his music, and to answering specific questions about the role and importance of music in human society.

Research in ethnomusicology normally involves two quite different activities—laboratory work and field work. At one time, anthropologists, folklorists, missionaries, or travelers collected music in the "field" and delivered their recordings to the musicologist for transcription and analysis in the laboratory. But the days of the "armchair" ethnomusicologist are over, and it is now assumed each scholar will do his own field and laboratory work. The complex questions of today's research projects, in fact, demand that the scholar gain the insights which only come from firsthand experiences and observations in the field. This variety—the constant alternation between field work and laboratory work, the opportunity for close dealings with people, often of another culture, and, in many cases, the chance to teach and to write—is why ethno-musicologists find their field not only challenging but enjoyable.

Field work is a rather arduous and specialized task, involving more than simply finding a band of Indians and switching on the tape recorder. It requires knowledge of the kinds of data needed to answer the specific research questions; it demands an intimate acquaintance with the language and culture of the informants; it calls for a great deal of patience, understanding, and an ability to relate to other people, resembling a combination of public relations and psychic intuition. Maturity is needed on the part of the researcher, who must often spend many long months away from his own culture, immersed in a foreign one.

Many types of field projects are possible. One can investigate the music of a specific group: a village community, a city block, a particular school or church. One can study the musical background, knowledge, and life history of an individual, or conduct research on a special musical genre. Projects sometimes focus on specific problems, for instance, the impact of a developing record industry on the musical life of a town, or the effect introduction of transistor radios has on the music of a village. Or research can center on the musical results of contact between different cultural groups, for instance the impact of Western culture on the music of an American Indian community or changes that Italian folk music undergoes in an American urban environment.

Several methods are commonly used for gathering data in the field. Information may be elicited directly from informants by asking questions informally, conducting formal interviews, distributing questionnaires, or even administering special tests. Scholars may participate in the culture by joining in the daily round of activities, by learning to sing in the local style or play an instrument, or by actually performing music with informants. And a scholar may make observations from his perspective as an outsider. Most researchers use all these techniques in some combination to gather their data, taking the role of a "participant-observer" in the culture under study.

Often the specific goals of a research project require the recording of musical events as they occur or the elicitation of certain musical items for recording. In the past, before the advent of the phonograph, scholars tried to write down the music as they heard it performed in the field, but this is usually so difficult that even several repeated hearings are not sufficient for an accurate notation. There is an amusing (though perhaps spurious) story about a great German anthropologist who was doing field work in Australia. He knew nothing about music, but he heard a native song that he thought interesting, and he wished that he could somehow transport it to his musicological colleagues. Since no recording apparatus was available, he proceeded to memorize the song. But his musical memory was poor, and he decided to rehearse the song every day so he would not forget it. By the time he returned to Europe and sang it for his colleagues, they laughed, because it sounded just like a German popular song. Because he was not acquainted with the native system of music and perceived it only by comparing it with his own, he had gradually and unconsciously changed the song to conform to his own ideas and tastes and to what had been his musical experience.

Today's standard collecting equipment is the tape recorder, both reel-to-reel and cassette; in the past, collectors have used Edison cylinders (some early ones operated by a treadle similar to that of a sewing machine), then aluminum and acetate disks, and since World War II, wire. Tape recording did not become popular in the United States until the early 1950's, although it has been used longer in Germany, where the first collection of folk music on tape was probably Fritz A. Bose's work on German folk ballads in 1936.[1] For best acoustic results, tape should move as fast as possible past the recording head. Unfortunately, speed increases considerably the amount of tape needed (and therefore the cost). A rate of 7½ inches per second is sufficiently fast for recording music, 15 inches practically ideal. For recording interviews or other speech, 3¾ is satisfactory; cassette, because of its light weight and easy portability, is preferable.

No general formula for successful recording can be offered, as the requirements of each project vary, and some projects, particularly those concentrating on the function of music in its cultural context, may not require any recording. Much folk music known today—the Child ballads, the music of some American Indian tribes, and that of European groups in rural America—was collected using certain procedures that have characterized most folkloric collecting of the first half of the twentieth century.

First, the collector usually tries to find an informant who is considered an authority on folk music in his community (and often one, if possible, who has not spent much time outside his culture). He should be persuaded to sing as many songs as he knows, even if some are fragmentary. Often such a person in rather old and his voice will not be as good as in the past; but that he knows much material and remembers a bygone era makes him a worthwhile informant for old songs. Then the collector should find other persons and collect from them whatever they know, especially including, if possible, the same material as that collected from the first informant. Scholars have generally tried to record the same songs from several people because slight differences among the various versions occur. Finally, the collector returns to all of his informants and asks them to perform again the material sung earlier. This is necessary because there may be important differences between the versions, differences that are interesting from a number of points of view. For example, we may assume that certain features of a performance are significant and meaningful to performer and listener, and others are insignificant and arbitrary, and might as well not be there. A performer usually leaves intact the significant features, but he may change the insignificant ones. The study of various renditions of the same music by one or several performers may enable scholars to discover the essentials of a music, which elements are important in a given style and which are not.

Re-recording sometimes presents unforeseen problems. Some of the Plains Indian tribes, many of whose songs use nonlexical syllables instead of words, do not identify the songs by name. As a result one cannot always ask a singer to perform a specific song. A song can be identified by its use; for example, it can be called a love song or a Rabbit Dance song, but these are categories and would make the singer think of a large group of songs. The collector can sing the beginning of the song he wants to hear, or play a bit of a previous recording, but this in a way defeats the purpose of re-recording because the informant's mind is directed to what he has just heard, and the dice are loaded in favor of that particular version. Since there is often no lexical text, it cannot be quoted. Sometimes the only recourse is simply to ask the singer to sing all the songs he sang before, and hope that he will faithfully do so. Even then unscrambling the recordings, to identify the variants and the performances that go together, can be a problem, for in many repertories all the songs sound very much alike to Western ears; and two separate songs may sometimes seem even closer to us than two versions of a single song. This is one of the many intricacies and fascinations of studying folk music.

This collecting procedure characterizes research on songs that in the past have been considered "authentic" music— the oldest, presumably unchanging items of a repertory, those songs that were considered "pure" reflections of the spirit of the culture, music not influenced by popular styles or by the music of neighboring cultures. Consequently, scholars sought old people in the community, the guardians of the "genuine" tradition, for information on music.

The notion of a culture having only one authentic music has been rejected by most ethnomusicologists today. Folk and tribal societies are able to learn and produce several musical styles. Most scholars now feel that all music of a culture—old songs as well as new ones, songs that show influences of another culture as well as those that do not—are worthy of study. And, in fact, most musical styles in today's world are hybridized and "nonauthentic." As a result, collecting procedures must vary in different research projects: if one wants to investigate the role of music in adolescent groups, it clearly would not make sense to interview only the old men of the village.

Besides making recordings, the researcher should also take thorough field notes. A collection of tapes is of no value without adequate documentation. The field worker must note the name of each song, the number of versions that have been recorded, and the date of recording. The type and use of each song should be reported and if possible its function in the society. The informant should be asked how he learned each song and when. General information about the musical culture of the group is also essential; for instance, who composes songs, and how; what terms are used to describe music; what status do musicians have in the society; how is music taught and learned; and what is the native classification of musical types? Standards of performance are also of great interest, for these vary from culture to culture. For example, the Plains Indians prefer high voices, but the Pueblo Indians of the Southwest prefer low, growling voices. The collector should find out which singers are regarded as the best performers and why they are considered superior. He should gather information about musical instruments, their construction, use, and tuning. A rule of thumb: any statements about music made by native informants are welcome, and may prove important and relevant to the research questions.

In the laboratory, for the purpose of analysis, the researcher may need to transcribe part or all of his collection into musical notation. Again, needs vary from project to project, and not all research problems require transcription; for others, detailed transcription is essential. Transcribing a piece of traditional music is a difficult job. It is sometimes so time-consuming that it is not uncommon for a song that takes one minute to perform to be transcribed only after an hour or more of work. Why should it take so long if, after all, first-year college music students learn to write down what they have heard repeated three or four times, in exercises called "dictation"? The reason points up one of the important and interesting facts about methods of studying folk music.

There are at least two ways of reducing what one hears to notation. One can expect to hear music in a preconceived pattern, as in classes of music theory, where students are taught what to listen for, and then to supplement what they have actually heard with what they know probably will be played next. But the student of folk music has a different point of view. He must write down exactly what occurs in the music; he must not allow his hearing to be diverted by preconceived ideas of what should take place. Otherwise what he writes will be subjective, influenced by the kind of music he has been used to hearing, and he will "correct" what he hears in the light of his previous listening, creating a transcription that obviously would not tell us about the music itself, only about the student's reaction to it.

As members of Western European culture, we have been conditioned since childhood to a type of music that is complex and specialized, with an accompanying theory that tells us it is the best and highest type of music. When we listen to the music of other cultures, our natural tendency is to compare it to our own music and to correct in our minds the sounds we hear with our ears, so they will conform to our ideas. But the non-Western systems of music, and those of folk music, are often quite different from ours, with different patterns in melody, rhythm, harmony. Since folk music often uses other scales, the pitches cannot always be reproduced on our instruments. And since our system of notation has evolved out of Western music, it is often difficult, if not impossible, to use it for transcribing the music of other cultures.

Some mechanical devices have been developed that are much more accurate in transcription than the human ear.

These, however, only give us a partial insight into the music. Electronic apparatus can notate the acoustic aspects of music, vibration rates and overtones, and thus, does have its value.

The oscillograph records all the pitches and overtones of a piece on a rotating drum with a stylus (much like a thermometer that records temperatures over a period of time). What it writes is very difficult to decipher because it includes so much more than the human ear can perceive. Oscillograph print-outs must be re-transcribed into conventional notation to be useful in most cases.

The stroboscope is more helpful, but it does not transcribe. It simply measures the exact pitch of a tone. It can aid in determining the scale of a piece, but it would be an endless task to attempt to use a stroboscope for every note of a song. For uncertain or especially interesting pitches and intervals, however, it is of great value.

Some attempts at an "instantaneous" music notator, into which recordings would be "fed" and digested into finished transcriptions of a highly technical nature, have not yet resulted in a model for general consumption. The most promising ones—called melographs—have been developed by Charles Seeger, and by scholars at Hebrew University in Jerusalem, designed to supplement rather than replace the human ear.[2]

Since music is, after all, performed by and for humans, the best instrument for recording it is, in spite of its limitations, the human ear and mind. But the ear should be careful not to superimpose its own cultural and musical experience on what it hears. The transcriber has to be prepared to hear distinctions in pitch that do not exist, or rather that are not significant in his own musical culture, and he must expect to hear rhythmic combinations and complexities beyond those he knows. To accommodate differences between folk or non-Western music and Western music, some special signs are used with our system of notation.

The following symbols are most frequently used to represent features in folk music foreign to Western notation:

+, ↑   slightly higher than notated
⌐, ↓   slightly lower than notated
(♩)   uncertain pitch
⌐   indefinite pitch
✗   grace note, without rhythmic value
ụ,ị ị weak tones
P̈   pulsations
⌒̣   strong tie
⌒̂ ̂   glissando
⌒   slightly longer than notated
⌣   slightly shorter than notated

Some of the schemes for notating folk music modify the staff system in favor of a different arrangement of lines. The use of graph paper, which can show note length and pitch variation, seems promising for some purposes. Another method uses a conventional staff of large proportions, which enables the transcriber to place the notes at various points between the lines and spaces:

Frances Densmore has tried writing Indian songs in simplified form by representing only the over-all melodic contour.[3] The difficulty with these methods is that most people learn to read conventional music notation with a certain amount of effort, after which they are not amenable to learning other methods. While these special schemes do have some value for presenting material to specialists and students, it seems best for the general reader and for educational purposes to continue with the conventional system aided by these special modifications.

In any case, transcriptions are merely symbols, approximations of sound. It would be difficult for a Westerner to take such a transcription, to sing or play it, and have it sound at all like the original performance. Nevertheless, transcriptions are useful and sometimes necessary for learning about folk music, for it is difficult to analyze music from the sound recordings alone.

The analysis of folk music is a complex and difficult process that requires advanced knowledge of music theory. The following basic principles, however, distinguish analysis from research in other kinds of music. Since the scholar who analyzes folk music is often working in a medium relatively distant from the music most familiar to him, he must be extremely careful, just as in transcribing, not to impose his own ideas and experiences on the music. He must not give way to the temptation of calling unusual intervals out-of-tune equivalents of their Western counterparts, or of calling complex rhythmic patterns "free" or "chaotic." He should abstain from criticizing and evaluating his material from an aesthetic point of view, since this is likely to distort the analysis and to produce an ethnocentric, thus irrelevant, judgment.

As knowledge about folk music of the world has expanded, the resources and techniques for its study have expanded as well. Tape recording is no longer the only way to gather data in the field. Film and video tape recording are important tools for many research projects, particularly "micro-ethnographic" studies—in-depth investigations of all aspects of one musical event. With the increasing use of computers, transcription is no longer regarded as the inevitable first step in the analysis of folk music.

Ethnomusicology is becoming increasingly interdisciplinary; the field today includes a multiplicity of approaches and many schools of thought. Most notable of recent developments in musical analysis is the use of concepts from linguistics, both the structural linguistics of Roman Jakobson and transformational grammar. Many scholars claim that the rules governing language resemble the rules governing music. Music systems and language systems do share common characteristics; both music and language have elements that are significant and other elements that, because they are predictable or devoid of specific symbolism, are less significant. Musical systems, like language systems, can perhaps be described by a small number of basic rules and operations (as in a transformational grammar).

Today's ethnomusicologist needs to take a broad view of his field. Fifty years ago it may have been acceptable to outline one "best" method for studying the music of all cultures, but any such general prescription is no longer of great value. Each group, each society, each culture presents its own unique problems. In many repects, the researcher is required to develop a tailor-made method for his investigation—an approach that suits the questions he seeks to answer.

XI

FOLK MUSIC
AND THE PROFESSIONAL SINGER

Most readers have probably had their first contact with folk song from recordings made by professional folk singers. It was recently suggested to a student that he collect some folk songs for a term project, whereupon he asked whether the instructor knew anyone who could get him a discount at a local record store. For him, folk songs existed only on commercial records, sung by professionals. He was unaware that he himself knew some folk songs, learned from his mother, and that, as far as the social context was concerned, folk music was in any way different from cultivated and popular music. It is important to realize that what the professional folk singer is doing, is trying to do, and in fact is required to do is quite different from what the member of the folk community does.

Folk music usually undergoes some very fundamental changes when it becomes part of an urban or a collegiate musical culture. Some of these changes are obvious, others subtle. But the lover of folk music should be aware of them, and be careful not to confuse the two modes of presentation. Their confusion has often resulted in misrepresentation of facts concerning the original, rural form; on the other hand, it has led to considerable abuse being heaped on the professional folk singer.

If we assume, as we have throughout this book, that a song may be folk music under some circumstances and cultivated music under other circumstances, it is possible that songs sung by the professionals are not, and cannot be, genuine folk songs. In order to solve this dilemma, we would have to decide whether a piece of music can exist in an abstract form, outside of a performance. The answer for folk music could easily be "No," because oral tradition is its primary distinguishing feature. Since folk music proper lives only in performance, we can judge it only within its medium of presentation.

The professional's degree of knowledge and firsthand experience in folklore varies from person to person. Some professionals are members of a genuine folk tradition, of families in which oral culture is well established. They usually embark on professionalism through urbanization, and they are affected accordingly. For example, an informant who sang for Library of Congress collectors decided that he was successful enough among those learned gentlemen to go to New York and become a full-time ballad singer. Other folk singers come from the field of classical music; they are trained concert artists who like folk songs and wish to bring them to their audiences. Others again, are scholars with a knack for public performance and entertainment. Some professionals have a thorough knowledge of the fundamentals of folklore and the factors that separate it from other types of tradition; still others constantly exhibit incredible naiveté (or arrogance) and are willing to call practically everything they wish to sing a folk song.

The presentation of folk songs by professional singers is a force to be reckoned with in today's urban musical culture.

Its over-all influence has certainly been beneficial to the survival of folk music at large, in spite of the misunderstandings to which it has exposed its subject. It has caused a boom in the cities, which has in turn reached the whole country and persuaded the usual bearers of folk tradition to renew their waning enthusiasm. The purposes of professional folk singers are usually laudable, for they are concerned with fostering a deeper understanding of folk heritage. Too often, however, the professional has been propelled by political and nationalist ideas. In various European countries, especially Nazi Germany, Fascist Italy, and the Communist states, folk music has been used to further the desires of the government, to underscore false scientific theories, and for other propaganda purposes. Whether the actions of these governments are in themselves acceptable or not, this use of folk music has resulted in widespread misinformation about the nature of folklore and folk culture, and the song material itself has suffered from changes imposed by the state. The American government has not participated in this subversion of folk music. But among the professional folk singers are some who have used their material with such aims in mind. The use of folk music by professionals and its appreciation widely by intellectual audiences date from the late 1920's, when songs were used to underscore the movements for social justice and to give emotional appeal to the arguments of labor. Later the use of folk music shifted from the "folks of the left" (Woodie Guthrie, for example) to those of "the right," and folk song became a patriotic and even nationalistic expression. Some folk singers tried to show the alleged superiority of Anglo-American folk songs over those of other ethnic groups, and Americanization of minority groups via folk music was attempted.

Even when such motives are not involved, as in the majority of cases, it seems to be practically impossible for the professional folk singer to present his songs in a way that gives a true picture of the musical folk culture of the United States. After all, he is singing for the entertainment of an audience. In the folk culture the songs have a function beyond aesthetic enjoyment, but in the city this function may be lost, and the folk singer must compete with Beethoven and Hoagy Carmichael for the favors of an audience. It is a sophisticated audience that knows what it wants. And it usually does not want folk songs served in the austere way of the countryside; it wants music that adheres to the prevalent tastes and fads, with a little of that folksiness and quaintness which the urbanites believe to be characteristic of folklore. The professional folk singer must cater to these wishes if he is to be successful. And from this need stem the various characteristics of professional folk singing, traits that are far removed from those of genuine folk music.

The professional folk singer inevitably accompanies his songs with an instrument, since cultivated music is prevailingly accompanied. But in order to give the appearance of authenticity, he uses folk instruments, or what resembles them. The guitar and the banjo are most common, and often they are perfectly in place. Only when the accompaniment takes on the character of a solo performance, when it is played with virtuosity, does it cease to sound like folk music. But sophisticated audiences are usually not content with simple accompaniments, restricted to prosaic strumming of two or three chords. They want some "razzle-dazzle," and the performer supplies it. Other folk instruments, the dulcimer, the mandolin, and the zither, have been constructed and are played with greater complexities than they ever are in a folk community. Instruments of the Renaissance, the lute and the recorder, have been resurrected by folk singers, although these instruments were mainly part of a sophisticated musical culture and are not from the folk. All of this is good entertainment, even good music, but it is an entirely different phenomenon from the folk music discussed earlier in this book. And it may give the listener a completely false impression of what his folk heritage is.

The trap into which the professional folk singer frequently falls is the individualization to which he must subject his songs and the attention which he must draw to himself as their interpreter. American folk culture does not admit such individuality. While songs do have interpretations characteristic of individual singers, a singer in a folk culture sticks close to his tradition, in spite of the effects of communal re-creation. His person is not the center of the listener's attention, for he is only the temporary mouthpiece of a long tradition in which the individual rendition is only incidental. The professional or collegiate folk singer must focus attention on himself because his audience insists upon it. This audience wants to hear an individual, not a tradition, the peculiarities and mannerisms of an interpreter, not the characteristics of a widespread style and its culture. The professional must sing his songs in a special, inimitable way, he must rehearse his peculiarities, and he must arrive at a distinct version of each song, a version which then has to ossify so that it will remain the same for years; if it changes, the audience will think its hero is "slipping." He must practice his trademarks, his way of removing his coat, his talking to the audience. Obviously these traits are completely contradictory to the style of genuine folk music. There is nothing wrong with them in themselves; indeed, they are the essentials of cultivated music, but they give a false picture of folklore, and the listener should be aware of the discrepancy.

Genuine folk singers who become entertainers in urban civilization take on the characteristics of professionals even though they begin as members of a folk community. This is true even of some American Indian singers who entertain tourists; they begin to concentrate on one style of singing and on one kind of song—what the tourists find most appealing and believe to be characteristically Indian. Folk singers select those melodies that allow them to exhibit vocal brilliance and virtuosity. The use of harmony and other kinds of part-singing in Anglo-American songs is common in the professional repertory but rare in folk cultures.

There are many other ways in which professional singers change the musical characteristics of the raw material. Their

greatest offense is the introduction of songs into their so-
called "folk" repertory that are not folk songs; they may be
cultivated or popular songs, or songs the folk singer has
composed himself. Why this indulgence? Again, because
genuine folk songs may not be sufficiently entertaining and
do not always conform to the notions of quaintness and
folksiness the city audience believes essential in folklore.
The professional must supply the public's wants and has had
to go far afield to find the right product. He has used cultivated medieval music, which, so far as we know, was never a
part of folklore. He sings patriotic songs, labor songs, work
songs which were never in oral tradition. Evidently, the
professional folk singer is committed to a career of mixed
purposes, and the good, musical, sophisticated arrangements
he makes of folk songs, the interpretations that are often
interesting and penetrating, must be presented as folklore if
they are to sell. A few professionals have solved this problem
by calling themselves arrangers, and some have tried to
explain what they are doing in scholarly and objective terms.
But most of them persist in defeating the educational aims to
which they are often devoted, because they are not willing to
tell their audiences what they are doing and how their
versions differ from those of folk culture proper.

Professional singing is most common in the Anglo-
American and Afro-American traditions, but is also evident in
the musical cultures of most American ethnic groups. For
ethnic groups, it is largely a method of preserving the songs
and, more particularly, of fostering national pride and unity.
Again, laudable as these aims may be in themselves, they
may give a biased picture of folk music.

Today, folk music concerts take place in cities and on
campuses. Professional folk singers such as Bob Dylan and
Joan Baez have been in the forefront of the popular scene.
Folk festivals have been sponsored by universities and other
cultural organizations such as the Smithsonian Institution, as
well as by less prestigious groups, and they are attended by
tens of thousands.

The public interest in folk music in America has changed since the 1950's. While popular folk singers have given rise to such genres as folk rock—combining folk music with popular styles—recently older, less modernized, folk styles have also come to the urban population. A number of rural singers and instrumentalists, who in earlier times would not dream of this sort of exposure, have been attracted to the concert stage and have given seminars and workshops at universities. No doubt, the folk musicians who participate in this kind of activity are exceptional; they are the ones who found it emotionally and psychologically possible to appear in front of large audiences, or to discuss their work with people who are, in some ways, of another culture.

The most important recent phenomenon rising from the folk is the music of singers such as Judy Collins or Joni Mitchell, much of which has only tenuous connections with the rural folk songs of Appalachia or which such folkloristic classics as the Child ballads. There are several reasons for the inclusion of this repertory in a discussion of folk music. The singers do occasionally make use of older, more traditional folk songs, thereby keeping the connection intact. The style of the majority of their songs, however, is not close to rural folk music or to country and western music, but neither is it related very closely to popular music such as rock. The character of the guitar accompaniment relates these songs to folk music, and, curiously enough, the character of the words (whose structure and content fit the nonnarrative genres of folk music quite well) often has more to do with nineteenth- and twentieth-century art songs than with any other style. In the musical conceptualization of the contemporary public, however, Mitchell, Collins, and Simon and Garfunkel are regarded as folk singers because of the musical style of the tunes and their accompaniment, because the audience feels that the music speaks to anyone of any age, and because these singers also include some "true" folk songs in their repertories.

Professional folk singing for entertainment is a great preservative: it is also a catalytic agent. While preserving folk-lore, it changes its essence. Today, much of the appeal of professional folk music in the United States comes because these songs remind us of the past, of less complicated times in which there was still a rural culture. But in order to find out about the true heritage of song in the United States we must go into the field, to the folk singer for whom songs are not only entertainment but also the expression of a way of life.

XII

FOLK MUSIC
AND THE COMPOSER

The use of folk music by the composers of cultivated or so-called art music has been an important factor in the history of music. Composers have usually felt closer to, and more familiar with, folk music than have the historians of cultivated music, and, indeed, virtually all our knowledge of folk music before the nineteenth century comes directly from sources of cultivated music rather than from theoretical and historical writing. In the early epochs of Western history, folk and cultivated music were probably more similar in style and more clearly related in function than they are today. There was evidently a time in European culture when there was no essential distinction between the two types; the increasing degree of differentiation may have come about simply through the growing professionalism and specialization among composers.

The earliest relationship between traditional and cultivated music is probably that in an individual ethnic or

national group. Professional composers began using traditional elements unconsciously, without feeling that they
were dealing with something foreign to their usual musical
experience. They combined the similar styles used by the
two groups without feeling that they were borrowing from
one and adding to the other. The background for this similar-
ity is usually the common musical heritage and experience
and the sharing of a common culture. Today, as in times past,
the cultivated music in a country derives from the same
undifferentiated tradition as the folk music. This situation
may explain the relatively free and informal use of folk music
by professional composers before the nineteenth century,
composers who evidently considered folk music a part of
their own tradition rather than a related but basically different one. Interest in folk music grew tremendously in the
nineteenth century, and traditional material began then to be
set apart, so to speak, and treated in a special way.

Since about 1800, professional composers have used folk
and even tribal music, but they have viewed it as something
exotic. Composers have not always integrated such materials
into their styles, but simply added both elements as if these
parts could be removed again without disturbing the results
of their own personal inspiration. Their use of folk music can
be arranged in three categories:

1. *Using folk melodies without essential changes.* This
usually consists of harmonizations of folk songs with accompaniment sometimes intended to bring out the "folk style,"
and at other times evidently composed to hide the peculiarities of that style and make the song conform to the standards
of cultivated music. The one method, delineating the folk
style, is exemplified by Béla Bartók's harmonizations of Hungarian, Slovak, and Rumanian folk songs; the other method,
conforming the folk style to other standards, is shown in the
Irish, Scottish, and Welsh songs of Beethoven. In all of these,
the folk melodies remain undisturbed in their original form,
and the composer has contributed a harmonic setting, in-
spired, in the case of Bartók, by the songs themselves, and in

Beethoven's arrangements, by the composer's own style of harmony.

2. *Using folk melodies that have been changed somewhat to conform with the system and structure of cultivated music.* Examples of this category are found most commonly where the traditional material is in a style considerably removed from the cultivated composer. In the American Indian songs used by American composers, for example, certain pitch differentiations cannot be reproduced easily on European instruments. The original Indian material may then be changed so that it can be played on the piano or by an orchestra. Changing the instrument without changing the music itself also comes under this category of arrangement. Similar changes may be made for rhythm and other elements of the music. A famous example of this type of folk song use is the second theme of the first movement of Tschaikowsky's *Fourth Symphony*, based on a folk song, "The Beech Tree."

3. *Composing music imitating a folk style.* This category is probably of the greatest interest and is the most common. Composition of folk-like music, often necessitating some analysis by the composer, ranges from individual motifs and themes to full-length symphonies, as well as such short forms as songs and instrumental character-pieces.

For a professional composer to become something of a folk-composer involves either saturation with a folk style through long contact with the members of a folk group or through musicological study. The results of such use of folk music are varied. Some composers write melodies in the style of folk songs and fit them into an environment that bears little or no relation to that style. This happened, for example, in Dvořák's *Fifth Symphony* (*From the New World*); the second theme of the first movement imitates an Indian song in a symphony that is otherwise not Indian in style. Another example may be a theme in Aaron Copland's *Appalachian Spring* that sounds like an American fiddle tune. That these discrepancies do not inhibit the general effectiveness of the compositions goes without saying.

Less frequently, composers have taken certain characteristic elements of a folk style, such as a peculiar kind of tonal
organization, a rhythmic pattern, or a melodic contour, and
used it, leaving other elements of the music in their nonfolk
style. An example is the violin solo from Rimsky-Korsakov's
Scheherazade, where the rhythmic monotony and the inter-
weaving of a few tones reminiscent of Arabic and Persian
music are incorporated in a Western tonal and harmonic
structure.

Some composers try to reproduce the stylistic features of
folk music even in those elements of their music that are not
present in the folk style at all, such as harmony. This feature
is usually accomplished by extending the patterns of the folk
style, such as using a scale in the harmony that is already
present in the melody. Imparting the elements of folk or
exotic music to the entire musical structure of a complex
Western piece has been used by some modern composers, for
example, by Bartók in Hungarian, and by Vaughan Williams
in English, folk songs.

The use of folk music has had several purposes. Occasionally it has been used to create a light or gay mood. In music
with a text or a program (representation of nonmusical material), rustic scenes and peasants are sometimes characterized
by folk-like elements. Local color and various geographic lo-
cations can be indicated by folk, or folk-like, music. In the
nineteenth century the main motivation for using traditional
material seems to have been the growing national consciousness among countries where the contribution to cultivated
music had hitherto been small: Russia (Moussorgsky, Rimsky-
Korsakov, Balakirev, Borodin), Denmark (Gade), England
(Vaughan Williams, Britten), Spain (De Falla, Albéniz), Ruma-
nia (Enesco), Bohemia (Smetana, Dvořák), Hungary (Liszt,
Bartók, Kodály), and others. It applies less to the centers of
Western musical culture, Germany, Austria, Italy, and France.
In these, composers often used folk music to illustrate the
rural aspects of culture and to symbolize the foreign or exotic,
a practice that has more recently become widespread. Thus

we have the *Capriccio Espagnol* of Rimsky-Korsakov (show-
ing he did not use Russian folk music alone), the use of Negro
and American Indian themes by Dvořák to show his reaction
to America, and the use of American Indian themes by American composers of English descent, and of Indonesian elements by Colin McPhee, an American.

In the late nineteenth and early twentieth centuries, some
composers used traditional music because it gave them opportunities to find new structural features and entire new musical
systems. Here the music itself often does not sound the least
bit like folk music. Modern composers who use microtones
and quartertones, like the Czech Alois Hába, were influenced
by the small intervals of Near Eastern music. Bartók's compositions contain structural principles found in many Hungarian
tunes, such as a characteristic symmetry in tonal structure,
even when folk style is not otherwise evident.

Whereas European folk music with styles closely related
to Western cultivated music has had an influence at home for
centuries, the more remote styles of tribal and oriental music
have become available to Western composers only recently.
Nevertheless, these styles have exercised a considerable influence during the last few decades.

American composers have used indigenous material in
their attempt to create a national American music, a musical
style to distinguish themselves from European composers.[1]
As members of a culture—Western—they first thought of
using the music of their own tradition, such as the English
and Scottish. But since this music is basically a European
importation, it did not distinguish them from their colleagues. So the American composers have turned to the folk
music which the United States shares with no other country,
American Indian and Afro-American songs. This material
predominates in American compositions.

It was actually a Czech composer—Dvořák—who first
championed American folk music and popularized the idea of
using Black folk songs, especially spirituals, as well as other
forms of American folk music in compositions. Dvořák had

great enthusiasm for all kinds of American folk music. In addition to the Afro-American elements suggested in the *New World Symphony,* he used themes based on American Indian music in his *Quartet* and *Quintet* for strings. Although he, unlike Bartók and De Falla, had little scientific knowledge about folk genres, his influence stimulated American composers to look to their own heritage for inspiration. Dvořák had many followers in America: William Arms Fisher, Rubin Goldmark, Harvey Worthington Loomis, and Henry Thacker Burleigh. The titles of Goldmark's orchestral works indicate the breadth of his interest in American folklore: *Hiawatha Overture, Negro Rhapsody, The Call of the Plains.*

Among the first composers interested in Indian materials was Edward MacDowell. His *Indian Suite,* first performed in 1896, was, in the composer's words, "suggested for the most part by melodies of the North American Indians."[2] The titles of the movements indicate some aspects of Indian culture: I, *Legend;* II, *Love Song;* III, *In War-time;* IV, *Dirge;* V, *Village Festival.* Another composer who used Indian material is Arthur Farwell; his compositions include *American Indian Melodies* (1901), *The Domain of Hurakan* (1902), *Impressions of the Wa-Wan Ceremony of the Omahas* (1906), *From Mesa and Plain* (1905), and *Navajo War Dance.* Arthur Nevin composed an opera, *Poia,* based on a legend of the Montana Blackfoot Indians. Other "Indianist" composers of the early twentieth century include Charles Wakefield Cadman (*Shanewis, The Sunset Trail, Thunderbird Suite*) and Charles Sanford Skilton (*Kalopin, The Sun Bride, Two Indian Dances, Suite Primeval, American Indian Fantasie, Sioux Flute Serenade*). The use of Indian elements is usually limited to certain simple melodies with scales like those of cultivated music. The rhythms and the over-all forms of Indian music, however, are rarely used. The "Indianist" movement was a passing phase in the history of American music and one that fell short of achieving the indigenous, national style these composers strove to capture.[3]

Afro-American music was a source for many composers in the early twentieth century. Black songs combine the virtue of being fairly close to the style of cultivated music, being derived from White spirituals, yet they are a unique American contribution to music. Black songs have recently been the basis of arrangements for vocal soloists and choirs and as parts of instrumental pieces. The Black composers William Grant Still and Henry Thacker Burleigh, the latter a pupil of Dvořák, are important in this field. The significance of Black folk music in the development of popular music and jazz is obvious. Indirectly it has also been used by many composers who assimilated the elements of jazz into their compositions. George Gershwin is the most prominent American to have done so. Europeans, including such twentieth-century greats as Igor Stravinsky and Darius Milhaud, have also used elements from jazz in their works. French-language Black Creole music from Louisiana was incorporated into the pieces of a Creole composer, Louis Moreau Gottschalk, who gained a considerable reputation in Europe.

Anglo-American folk songs have not been entirely neglected. Charles Ives quoted them as themes in a number of his works, including his symphonies. He tried in several instances to convey the feelings and sounds of the simple musical performances that took place in his boyhood home in Danbury, Connecticut. Snatches of ragtime, hymn tunes, and "quicksteps" are found in compositions of Ives, such as *Three Places in New England,* the *Second String Quartet,* and *A Symphony: Holidays.* Daniel Gregory Mason also experimented with folklore in some of his pieces, notably in *Folk Song Fantasy,* which is based on the song "Fanny Blair." In more recent years, Aaron Copland and Roy Harris have used the British folk song style and incorporated some songs directly into their works. Copland and Virgil Thomson also have written choral and solo arrangements of folk songs. Their motive was, again, the creation of distinctly American music. The folk music of other ethnic groups, however, has only rarely been absorbed into American cultivated music.

The United States has participated in the general revival of folk music as a source of inspiration for the composers of modern civilization. To be sure, a truly new, American style has not emerged from the revival, and it is unlikely that such a style could have been created simply through the use of folk music in a country where musical traditions are so diverse and new. Nevertheless, the movement has contributed to the American people's awareness of their folklore, Indian, Afro-American, and British, and as such it deserves the attention of the student of folk music.

NOTES

Chapter II. *Defining Folk Music*

   1. Julian von Pulikowski, *Geschichte des Begriffes Volkslied im musikalischen Schrifttum* (Heidelberg, 1933), illustrates this diversity.

   2. "Folklore," in Funk and Wagnall's *Standard Dictionary of Folklore, Mythology, and Legend* (New York, 1949), 1: 398–403.

   3. Halsey Stevens, *The Life and Music of Béla Bartók* (New York, 1953), pp. 21–27; Béla Bartók, *Hungarian Folk Music* (London, 1931).

   4. Wilhelm and Jacob Grimm, *Deutsche Mythologie* (Leipzig, 1835).

   5. Hans Naumann, *Grundzüge der deutschen Volkskunde* (Frankfurt, 1922).

   6. Franz Magnus Boehme, *Altdeutsches Liederbuch* (Leipzig, 1877), pp. xii–xiii.

   7. Phillips Barry, "Communal Recreation," *Bulletin of the Folk Song Society of the North East*, No. 5 (1933), pp. 4–6.

Chapter III. *The Uses and Styles of Folk Music*

   1. Theories on the functionality of folk and tribal music have been developed by George Herzog and are discussed in various papers mentioned in the bibliographical aids.

   2. Siegfried Nadel, "The Origins of Music," *Musical Quarterly* 16 (1930): 531–46.

   3. Karl Bücher, *Arbeit und Rhythmus* (Leipzig, 1924).

   4. Hugh Tracey, *Chopi Musicians* (Oxford, 1948).

   5. Bruno Nettl, "Stylistic Change in Folk Music," *Southern Folklore Quarterly* 17 (1953): 216–20.

Chapter IV. *Indian Music of the United States*

   1. See A. L. Kroeber, *The Arapho* (New York, 1902), pp. 418–21.

   2. Bruno Nettl, "Notes on Musical Composition in Primitive Culture," *Anthropological Quarterly* 27 (1954): 81–90.

   3. George Herzog, "Salish Music," in Marian Smith, ed., *Indians of the Urban Northwest* (New York, 1949), p. 107.

4. George Herzog, "Music in the Thinking of the American Indian," *Peabody Bulletin*, May 1938, p. 4.

5. *Ibid.*, p. 5.

6. Frances Densmore, *Cheyenne and Arapaho Music* (Los Angeles, 1930), p. 40.

7. Frances Densmore, *Nootka and Quileute Music* (Washington, 1939), p. 185.

8. Ruth Benedict, *Patterns of Culture* (New York, 1934).

9. George Herzog, "A Comparison of Pueblo and Pima Musical Styles," *Journal of American Folklore* 49 (1936): 333.

10. George Herzog, "Speech-Melody and Primitive Music," *Musical Quarterly* 20 (1934): 460–61.

11. Bruno Nettl, "Observations on Meaningless Peyote Song Texts," *Journal of American Folklore* 66 (1953): 161–64.

12. Bruno Nettl, "The Shawnee Musical Style," *Southwestern Journal of Anthropology* 9 (1953): 284.

13. Herzog, "Speech-Melody and Primitive Music."

14. Bruno Nettl, "Text-Music Relations in Arapaho Songs," *Southwestern Journal of Anthropology* 10 (1954): 192–99.

15. Bruno Nettl, *North American Indian Musical Styles* (Philadelphia, 1954).

Chapter V. *The British Tradition*

1. Variants of the ballads mentioned in this chapter can be found in the various collections listed in the bibliographic aids.

2. Béla Bartók, *Hungarian Folk Music* (London, 1931); George Herzog, "Song," in Funk and Wagnall's *Standard Dictionary of Folklore, Mythology, and Legend*, 2: 1041.

3. Francis James Child, *The English and Scottish Popular Ballads* (8 vols.; Boston, 1857–59).

4. Samuel P. Bayard, "Prolegomena to a Study of the Principal Melodic Families of British-American Folk Song," *Journal of American Folklore* 63 (1950): 1–44.

5. From *Bay State Ballads*, LP Record Fp47/2, Folkways Records.

6. *The Sacred Harp* (Nashville, 1968) is a reprint of the third edition (1860) of this hymnal that also contains a reprint of George Pullen Jackson's 1944 essay, "The Story of The Sacred Harp, 1844–1944."

Chapter VI. *Afro-American Music*

1. J. H. Kwabena Nketia, *The Music of Africa* (New York, 1974); John Storm Roberts, *Black Music of Two Worlds* (New York, 1972).

2. Henry Edward Krehbiel, *Afro-American Folksongs* (New York, 1914).

3. George Pullen Jackson, *White and Negro Spirituals* (New York, 1943).

4. Melville J. Herskovits, *The Myth of the Negro Past* (New York,

1941); Richard A. Waterman, "African Influence in American Negro Music," in Sol Tax, ed., *Acculturation in the Americas* (Chicago, 1952); Erich M. von Hornbostel, "American Negro Songs," *International Review of Missions* 15 (1926):748–53.

    5. Jackson, *White and Negro Spirituals.*

    6. Harold Courlander, *Negro Folk Music U.S.A.* (New York, 1963).

    7. Charles Keil, *Urban Blues* (Chicago, 1966).

    8. Courlander, *Negro Folk Music U.S.A.*, p. 132.

    9. Courlander, *Negro Folk Music U.S.A.*, p. 135.

    10. Michael Haralambos, "Soul Music and Blues: Their Meaning and Relevance in Northern United States Black Ghettos," in Norman E. Whitten, Jr., and John F. Szwed, eds., *Afro-American Anthropology: Contemporary Perspectives* (New York, 1970), pp. 367–83.

    11. Daniel G. Hoffman, "From Blues to Jazz," *Midwest Folklore* 5 (1955): 107–14.

Chapter VII. *Hispanic-American Folk Music*

    1. Gilbert Chase, *The Music of Spain*, 2nd rev. ed. (New York, 1958).

    2. John Donald Robb, *Hispanic Folk Songs of New Mexico* (Albuquerque, 1954).

    3. Américo Paredes, "The Mexican Corrido: Its Rise and Fall," in Mody C. Boadright, Wilson M. Hudson, and Allen Maxwell, eds., *Madstones and Twisters* (Dallas, 1958), pp. 91–105.

    4. Robb, *Hispanic Folk Songs of New Mexico*, p. 83.

    5. Américo Paredes and George Foss, "The *Décima Cantada* on the Texas-Mexican Border: Four Examples," *Journal of the Folklore Institute* 3 (1966): 91–115.

    6. Vicente T. Mendoza, *La décima en México* (Buenos Aires, 1947).

    7. Américo Paredes, "The *Décima* on the Texas-Mexican Border: Folksong as an Adjunct to Legend," *Journal of the Folklore Institute* 3 (1966): 154–67.

    8. Robb, *Hispanic Folk Songs of New Mexico;* Chase, *The Music of Spain;* see also *Western Folklore* 16 (1957), *Los Pastores* Number.

    9. Robb, *Hispanic Folk Songs of New Mexico*, p. 70.

    10. Adelaida Reyes-Schramm, "The Role of Music in the Interaction of Black Americans and Hispanos in New York City's East Harlem," Ph.D. diss., Columbia University, 1975.

    11. Shulamith Rybak, "Puerto Rican Children's Songs in New York," *Midwest Folklore* 8 (1958): 5–20.

    12. Reyes-Schramm, "The Role of Music in the Interaction of Black Americans and Hispanos in New York City's East Harlem."

    13. I am grateful to Barbara Rehm of Brown University for her assistance in providing current data on music in the New England Portuguese colonies. For a history of these colonies see Rehm, "A Study of the Cape Verdean Morna in New Bedford, Massachusetts," M.A. the-

sis, Brown University, 1975; also Maud Cuney Hare, "Portuguese Folk-Songs from Provincetown, Cape Cod, Mass.," *Musical Quarterly* 24 (1938): 35–53.

14. Susan Terry Ferst, "The Immigration and the Settlement of the Portuguese in Providence: 1890–1924," M.A. thesis, Brown University, 1972; Laurinda Candida Andrade, *The Open Door* (New Bedford, Mass., 1968).

15. Rodney Gallop, "The Fado," *Musical Quarterly* 19 (1933): 200–213; John M. Reed, "The Fado," *American Record Guide* 32 (1966): 1044–47.

16. Rehm, "A Study of Cape Verdean Morna in New Bedford, Massachusetts."

Chapter VIII. *European Folk Music in Rural America*

1. Bruno Nettl, "The Hymns of the Amish: An Example of Marginal Survival," *Journal of American Folklore* 70 (1957): 323–28.

2. Don Yoder, *Pennsylvania Spirituals* (Lancaster, Pa., 1961); George Korson, ed., *Pennsylvania Songs and Legends* (Philadelphia, 1949).

3. Yoder, *Pennsylvania Spirituals*, p. 13. Copyright © 1961 by the Pennsylvania Folklore Society. Reprinted by permission.

4. Cecilia Ray Berry, ed., *Folk Songs of Old Vincennes* (Chicago, 1946).

5. Irene Therese Whitfield, *Louisiana French Folk Songs* (Baton Rouge, 1939).

6. Lucie de Vienne, "Notes," for "Cajun Songs from Louisiana," Ethnic Folkways Library Recording FE 4438, 1957.

7. Theodore C. Blegen and Martin B. Ruud, *Norwegian Emigrant Songs and Ballads* (Minneapolis, 1936); Einar Haugen, "Norwegian Emigrant Songs and Ballads," *Journal of American Folklore* 51 (1938): 69–75.

8. Arne Bjørndal, "The Hardanger Fiddle," *Journal of the International Folk Music Council* 8 (1956): 13–15.

9. Korson, *Pennsylvania Songs and Legends*, p. 91.

Chapter IX. *Folk Music in the City*

1. The folklore of the Detroit area has been extensively collected by Thelma G. James and her students at Wayne State University, especially in the field of oral literature and folk beliefs. Some collections and studies of music have been included in their project. In preparing the present chapter we have used these as well as material gathered by Nettl and by his students. This includes recorded songs and written song-texts, in the original as well as translation, with background information on songs and informants. The following ethnic groups were included: native Whites and Negro, German, Polish, Czech, Italian, Armenian, Scottish, Greek, Albanian, Russian, and Hungarian. In addition, we have used a Master's thesis by Helen Goranowski, "An Analysis of 65 Polish Folk Songs," Wayne University, 1951. An important publication resulting from

the collecting program at Wayne is Harriet M. Pawlowska, ed., *Merrily We Sing: 105 Polish Folksongs* (Detroit, 1961). Also Bruno Nettl and Ivo Moraveik, "Czech and Slovak Songs Collected in Detroit," *Midwest Folklore* 6 (1956): 37–49.

2. For Detroit, these groups are listed among the official and semi-official organizations of the ethnic groups in a detailed listing by Albert Mayer, "Ethnic Groups in Detroit: 1951" (Detroit, 1951), mimeographed.

3. Jacob A. Evanson, "Folk Songs of an Industrial City," in George Korson, ed., *Pennsylvania Songs and Legends* (Philadelphia, 1949), pp. 423–66.

Chapter X. *Studying Folk Music*

1. Fritz Bose, personal communication in 1955.

2. The UCLA Institute of Ethnomusicology, *Selected Reports in Ethnomusicology* 2, no. 1 (1974), is devoted to the Seeger Melograph Model C and its use in analysis of both vocal and instrumental pieces.

3. Frances Densmore, *Teton Sioux Music* (Washington, 1918).

Chapter XII. *Folk Music and the Composer*

1. The material in this chapter is partially based on two important general histories of American music, which also include thorough bibliographies: John Tasker Howard, *Our American Music* (New York, 1939), and Gilbert Chase, *America's Music*, 2nd rev. ed. (New York, 1966).

2. Howard, *Our American Music*, p. 331.

3. Chase, *America's Music*, pp. 400–401.

BIBLIOGRAPHIC AIDS

Suggestions for further reading and study

Chapter I

Introduction

A number of studies of various aspects of American folklore is given in Tristram P. Coffin, ed., *Our Living Traditions* (New York, 1968); and several studies of aspects of music in the Americas are collected in George List and Juan Orrego-Salas, *Music in the Americas* (The Hague, 1967).

Alan P. Merriam, "Music in American Culture," *American Anthropologist* 57 (1955): 1173–78, surveys briefly the unique structure of our musical life. Alan Lomax, *The Folk Songs of North America in the English Language* (New York, 1960), is mainly a collection of songs but includes important introductory comments about the nature of American folk music.

Chapter II

Defining Folk Music

There are not many books about folk music in general or about the definition and the concept of folk music. Several articles, especially that on "Folklore," in Funk and Wagnall's *Standard Dictionary of Folklore, Mythology, and Legend* (New York, 1949) can be recommended. For general introductions to ethnomusicology and the study of folk music, see Alan P. Merriam, *The Anthropology of Music* (Evanston, Ill., 1964); Bruno Nettl, *Theory and Method in Ethnomusicology* (New York, 1964); and Mantle Hood, *The Ethnomusicologist* (New York, 1971).

A number of important bibliographies, which list collections and studies, have been published. Among them should be mentioned Charles Haywood's *Bibliography of North American Folklore and Folksong* (New York, 2d rev. ed., 1961), which lists materials in Anglo-American, Indian, Negro, and all other groups; also Bruno Nettl, "Musicological Studies in American Ethnological Journals," *Notes* 13 (1955): 205–09. *A List of American Folksongs Currently Available on Records* was published by the Archive of American Folksong, Library of Congress, Washington, in 1953.

The standard bibliography of non-Western music is Jaap Kunst, *Ethnomusicology*, 3rd ed. (The Hague, 1959). A bibliography of current publications appears in each issue of *Ethnomusicology*, journal of the Society for Ethnomusicology.

Chapter III

The Uses and Styles of Folk Music

The function of folk music in society is discussed by George Herzog in the article, "Song," in Funk and Wagnall's *Standard Dictionary of Folklore, Mythology, and Legend* (New York, 1949), and in a series by Bruno Nettl in the various issues of *Etude*, 1956–1957. A short book by Russell Ames, *The Story of American Folk Song* (New York, 1955), gives a picture of American history as it appears in folk songs but deals only with the British tradition and makes little mention of the musical side of folk songs.

The variety and the common features of musical structure in European folk song are illustrated in an anthology, *Europäischer Volksgesang*, by Walter Wiora (Cologne, 1953). For a general survey of European folk music, see Bruno Nettl, *Folk and Traditional Music of the Western Continents*, 2nd ed. (Englewood Cliffs, N.J., 1973). See also Alan Lomax, *Folk Song Style and Culture* (Washington, 1968).

Tribal music has fared better, for there are several general accounts which cover all of the world's areas. Marius Schneider, "Primitive Music," in Vol. 1 of the *New Oxford History of Music* (London, 1957), and Bruno Nettl, *Music in Primitive Culture* (Cambridge, Mass., 1956), illustrate two contrasting viewpoints. Several books by Curt Sachs contain large sections on tribal music which show a third approach and tie their subject matter to European cultivated music in a unique way: *The Rise of Music in the Ancient World* (New York, 1943); *Rhythm and Tempo* (New York, 1953); and *World History of the Dance* (New York, 1937), which also, of course, discusses the relationship of tribal music to the dances of non-Western cultures.

Theories on the origin of music, relevant to a study of tribal music, are discussed in Siegfried Nadel, "The Origins of Music," *Musical Quarterly* 16 (1930): 531–46. A survey of primitive and folk instruments is included in Curt Sachs, *The History of Musical Instruments* (New York, 1940).

Chapter IV

Indian Music of the United States

Several survey studies of North American Indian music have been published. Helen H. Roberts, *Musical Areas in Aboriginal North America* (New Haven, 1936), and Bruno Nettl, *North American Indian Musical Styles* (Philadelphia, 1954), are the most recent. Among the collections of music without musicological discussions are *The Indians' Book* by Natalie Curtis-Burlin (New York, 1907) and the many books by Frances Densmore published by the Bureau of American Ethnology. The most important of Densmore's books are *Chippewa Music* (Washington, 1910); *Choctaw Music* (Washington, 1943); *Northern Ute Music* (Washington, 1922); *Papago Music* (Washington, 1929); and *Teton Sioux Music* (Washington, 1918). These also represent five distinct musical styles.

Among the studies of individual tribes, styles, and aspects of Indian music, the following are representative: Alice C. Fletcher, *The Hako* (Washington, 1904); George Herzog, "A Comparison of Pueblo and Pima Musical Styles," *Journal of American Folklore* 49 (1936): 283–417, and "The Yuman Musical Style," *Journal of American Folklore* 41 (1928): 183–231; David P. McAllester, *Peyote Music* (New York, 1949); Bruno Nettl, "Musical Culture of the Arapaho," *Musical Quarterly* 41 (1955): 325–31, and "The Shawnee Musical Style," *Southwestern Journal of Anthropology* 9 (1953): 277–85; Helen H. Roberts, *Form in Primitive Music* (New York, 1933); and Edward Sapir, "Song Recitative in Paiute Mythology," *Journal of American Folklore* 23 (1910): 455–72.

The relationship of music to other aspects of culture is discussed from various points of view in the following: George Herzog, "Music in the Thinking of the American Indian," *Peabody Bulletin*, May, 1938, pp. 1–5, and "Plains Ghost Dance and Great Basin Music," *American Anthropologist* 37 (1935): 403–19; David P. McAllester, *Enemy Way Music* (Cambridge, Mass., 1954); and Willard Rhodes, "Acculturation in North American Indian Music," in Sol Tax, ed., *Acculturation in the Americas* (Chicago, 1952). Willard Rhodes, "North American Indian Music, a Bibliographic Survey of Anthropological Theory," *Notes* 10 (1952): 33–45, classifies the many ways in which Indian music has been approached.

The most distinguished summary of the music of a single American Indian tribe published in recent years is Alan P. Merriam, *Ethnomusicology of the Flathead Indians* (Chicago, 1967). Among many studies of recent developments in North American Indian music, the best is Robert Witmer, "Recent Change in the Musical Culture of the Blood Indians," *Yearbook for Inter-American Musical Research* 9 (1973): 64–94.

Chapter V

The British Tradition

Two general introductory books must be mentioned first: Maud Karpeles, *An Introduction to English Folk Song* (London, 1973); and Roger D. Abrahams and George Foss, *Anglo-American Folksong Style* (Englewood Cliffs, N.J., 1968).

The ballad texts are listed, described, and annotated in four standard bibliographic works: Francis James Child, *The English and Scottish Popular Ballads* (5 vols. in 3; New York, 1957); Tristram P. Coffin, *The British Traditional Ballad in North America* (Philadelphia, 1951); Malcolm G. Laws, Jr., *Native American Balladry* (Philadelphia, 1951) and *American Balladry from British Broadsides* (Philadelphia, 1957).

A large number of printed collections are available; only a few are mentioned here, some of which contain material outside the Anglo-American tradition, particularly Negro folk songs: Benjamin A. Botkin, *The American Play-party Song* (Lincoln, Neb., 1937); Byron Arnold, *Folksongs of Alabama*

(University, Ala., 1950); Phillips Barry, Fannie H. Eckstrom, and Mary W. Smith, *British Ballads from Maine* (London, 1929); Samuel P. Bayard, *Hill Country Tunes* (Philadelphia, 1944), a collection of fiddle and fife tunes; Arthur Kyle Davis, *Traditional Ballads of Virginia* (Cambridge, Mass., 1929); Helen H. Flanders, *Ancient Ballads Traditionally Sung in New England* (Philadelphia, 1960–65); Emelyn E. Gardner and Geraldine J. Chickering, *Ballads and Songs of Southern Michigan* (Ann Arbor, 1939); George Pullen Jackson, *White Spirituals of the Southern Uplands* (Chapel Hill, 1933); George Korson, *Coal Dust on the Fiddle* (Philadelphia, 1943); John A. and Alan Lomax, *Cowboy Songs* (New York, 1938); Vance Randolph, *Ozark Folksongs* (Columbia, Mo., 1946–50); Franz Rickaby, *Ballads and Songs of the Shanty-Boy* (Cambridge, Mass., 1926); Ruth Crawford Seeger, *American Folk Songs for Children* (New York, 1948); and the most important, Cecil J. Sharp, *English Folk Songs from the Southern Appalachians* (London, 1932).

Much has been published in the way of criticism, analysis, and theory. Only a few items, indicating the different directions of research, are given here: Phillips Barry, *Folk Music in America* (New York, 1939); Samuel P. Bayard, "Decline and Revival of Anglo-American Folk Music," *Midwest Folklore* 5 (1955): 69–77, and "Prolegomena to a Study of the Principal Melodic Families of British-American Folk Songs," *Journal of American Folklore* 63 (1950): 1–44, both of which approach the entire body of Anglo-American folk music and treat it as a musical unit; Bertrand H. Bronson, "The Morphology of the Ballad Tunes," *Journal of American Folklore* 67 (1954): 1–14; Sigurd B. Hustvedt, *A Melodic Index of Child's Ballad Tunes* (Berkeley, 1936); Bruno Nettl, "The Musical Style of English Ballads Collected in Indiana," *Acta Musicologica* 27 (1955): 77–84; Cecil J. Sharp, *English Folk Song, Some Conclusions* (London, 1907); Evelyn Kendrick Wells, *The Ballad Tree* (New York, 1950). By far the most important study and compilation of the music of British ballads is Bertrand Harris Bronson, *The Traditional Tunes of the Child Ballads* (4 vols.; Princeton, 1959–72).

An excellent survey of collecting and scholarship is D. K. Wilgus, *Anglo-American Folksong Scholarship Since 1898* (New Brunswick, N.J., 1959).

Other aspects of Anglo-American folk music have been treated less consistently. As examples of the literature, we mention only George Pullen Jackson, *White Spirituals in the Southern Uplands* (Chapel Hill, 1933); Harold E. Cook, *Shaker Music, a Manifestation of American Folk Culture* (Lewisburg, Pa., 1973); and Archie Green, "Hear Those Beautiful Sacred Selections," *Yearbook of the International Folk Music Council* 1 (1970): 28–50.

Chapter VI

Afro-American Music

A large body of literature on Afro-American music exists, but much of it cannot be recommended from the point of view of authenticity and scholar-

ship. Among the collections, Edward A. McIlhenny, *Befo' de War Spirituals*
(Boston, 1933), N. I. White, *American Negro Folk-Songs* (Cambridge, Mass.,
1928), and George Pullen Jackson, *White and Negro Spirituals* (New York,
1954), are useful. In the field of description and theory, these are representative: E. M. von Hornbostel, "American Negro Songs," *International Review
of Missions* 15 (1926): 748–53; George Pullen Jackson, "The Genesis of the
Negro Spiritual," *American Mercury* 26 (1932): 243–48; Guy B. Johnson,
"The Negro Spiritual, a Problem in Anthropology," *American Anthropologist* 33 (1931): 157–71; Guy B. Johnson and H. W. Odum, *The Negro and His
Songs* (Chapel Hill, 1925); Henry E. Krehbiel, *Afro-American Folksongs*
(New York, 1914); Rudi Blesh, *Shining Trumpets* (New York, 1946); Richard
A. Waterman, "African Influences on American Negro Music," in Sol Tax,
ed., *Acculturation in the Americas* (Chicago, 1952), and "Hot Rhythm in
Negro Music," *Journal of the American Musicological Society* 1 (1948):
24–37.

During the late 1960's and 1970's, a vast body of literature exhibiting
entirely new viewpoints regarding the role of Afro-American music began to
appear. Examples of the most prominent publications: John Storm Roberts,
Black Music of Two Worlds (New York, 1972), is the best popular explana-
tion of the relationship among African, Afro-Latin, and North American
Black musics. The historical aspects are best treated in Eileen Southern, *The
Music of Black Americans* (New York, 1971) and *Readings in Black American Music* (New York, 1971). The role of music in Black society is touched
upon in several chapters of Norman E. Whitten, Jr., and John F. Szwed, eds.,
Afro-American Anthropology (New York, 1970). Charles Keil, *Urban Blues*
(Chicago, 1966), deals with blues and soul in the city environment.

Chapter VII

Hispanic-American Folk Music

For Spanish-American folk music, few collections exist, and the field
awaits extensive study. A general introduction is given in Gilbert Chase, *The
Music of Spain*, 2nd rev. ed. (New York, 1959), especially the chapters on
Iberian folk music, dance, and Hispanic music in the Americas. An invalu-
able bibliographic aid is Merle Simmons, *A Bibliography of the Romance
and Related Forms in Spanish America* (Bloomington, 1963). Fundamental
studies of the *romance* and *corrido* in New Mexico are Arturo L. Campa,
Spanish Folksong in the Southwest (Albuquerque, 1933), and *Spanish Folk-
Poetry in New Mexico* (Albuquerque, 1946). The *décima* tradition in Texas is
treated in Américo Paredes, "The *Décima* on the Texas-Mexican Border:
Folksong as an Adjunct to Legend," *Journal of the Folklore Institute*
(Indiana University) 3 (1966): 154–67; Paredes, *With His Pistol in His Hand:
A Border Ballad and Its Hero* (Austin, 1958); and Américo Paredes and
George Foss, "The *Décima Cantada* on the Texas-Mexican Border: Four

Examples," *Journal of the Folklore Institute* 3 (1966): 91–115. An older, but still useful study by a pioneering scholar of Hispanic culture in the Southwest is Charles F. Lummis, *The Land of Poco Tiempo* (New York, 1906), which includes both music and texts of a number of songs (Chapter IX); also Aurelio M. Espinosa, "Spanish Folk-Lore in New Mexico," *New Mexico Historical Review* 1 (1926): 135–55. Terrence L. Hansen, "Corridos in Southern California," *Western Folklore* 18, nos. 3, 4 (1959): 202–32, 295–315, gives thirty-three *corrido* texts with music and English translations.

For Hispanic music in New York, see two interesting but limited studies: Carlota Garfias, "Mexican Folklore Collected in New York City," *Journal of American Folklore* 51 (1938): 83–91; and Shulamith Rybak, "Puerto Rican Children's Songs in New York," *Midwest Folklore* 8 (1958): 5–20.

Music of the New England Portuguese has scarcely been investigated. An early article, "Portuguese Folk-Songs from Provincetown, Cape Cod, Mass.," by Maud Cuney Hare, *Musical Quarterly* 24 (1938): 35–53, should be mentioned.

Chapter VIII

European Folk Music in Rural America

The literature on the folk music of non-British immigrant groups to the United States is small. George Korson, *Pennsylvania Songs and Legends* (Philadelphia, 1949), includes some relevant material. A few publications are entirely devoted to non-British European immigrants: C. G. Peterson, *Creole Songs from New Orleans* (New Orleans, 1909); Bruno Nettl and Ivo Moravcik, "Czech and Slovak Songs Collected in Detroit," *Midwest Folklore* 5 (1955): 37–49; and Bruno Nettl, "The Hymns of the Amish, an Example of Marginal Survival," *Journal of American Folklore* 70 (1957): 323–28, which also gives other literature on German-American folk music. French-American folk music has hardly been studied, but Marius Barbeau, *Jongleur Songs of Old Quebec* (New Brunswick, N.J., 1962), treats a Canadian analogue. For Spanish-American folk music, few collections exist, and the field awaits extended treatment; but see Eleanor Hague, *Latin American Music, Past and Present* (Santa Ana, Calif., 1934).

Chapter IX

Folk Music in the City

The music of non-English-speaking minorities in American cities has been treated in several articles and books, for example: Harriet Pawlowska, *Merrily We Sing, 105 Polish Folk Songs* (Detroit, 1961); Stephen Erdely, "Folksinging of the American Hungarians in Cleveland," *Ethnomusicology* 8 (1964): 14–27; and several chapters in George Korson, *Pennsylvania Songs and Legends* (Philadelphia, 1949). See also Bruno Nettl, "Aspects of Folk Music in North American Cities," in List and Orrego-Salas, eds., *Music in the Americas* (Bloomington, 1967), 139–47; and Shulamith Rybak, "Puerto Rican Children's Songs in New York," *Midwest Folklore* 8 (1958): 5–20.

The following important collections of European folk music are perhaps relevant to this chapter: Béla Bartók, *Hungarian Folk Music* (London, 1931); Béla Bartók and Albert B. Lord, *Serbo-Croatian Folk Songs* (New York, 1951); Franz Magnus Boehme, *Altdeutsches Liederbuch* (Leipzig, 1877); Ludwig Erk and Franz Magnus Boehme, *Deutscher Liederhort* (Leipzig, 1859–1872); Boris Kremenliev, *Bulgarian-Macedonian Folk Music* (Berkeley and Los Angeles, 1952); Ilmari Krohn, *Suomen Kansan sävelmiä* (Helsinki, 1893–1912); A. E. Launis, *Lappische Juoigos-Melodien* (Helsinki, 1908); Elsa Mahler, *Altrussische Volkslieder aus dem Pecoryland* (Basel, 1951); John Meier, ed., *Deutsche Volkslieder mit thren Melodien* (Leipzig, 1935–59); Felipe Pedrell, *Cancionero musical popular español* (Barcelona, 1918); Kurt Schindler, *Folk Music and Poetry of Spain and Portugal* (New York, 1941).

Chapter X

Studying Folk Music

The methods of research in folk music and ethnomusicology in general are presented in several texts and surveys already mentioned in the bibliography of Chapter I: Alan P. Merriam, *The Anthropology of Music,* particularly Chapters 1–3; Mantle Hood, *The Ethnomusicologist,* Chapters 4–5; Bruno Nettl, *Theory and Method in Ethnomusicology,* Chapter 3. For folk music research specifically, see B. H. Bronson, *The Ballad as Song* (Berkeley, Calif., 1969). It is useful here to mention the most important periodicals in this field: *Ethnomusicology, Yearbook of the International Folk Music Council,* and *Journal of American Folklore.* All of them contain articles that explain methods of research as well as bibliographies.

Chapter XI

Folk Music and the Professional Singer

For information on individual folksingers and groups, see Lillian Roxon, *Rock Encyclopedia* (New York, 1969); and Ray Lawless, *Folksingers and Folksongs in America* (New York, 1960). Folk music as mass entertainment is discussed in several chapters of Charles Hamm, Bruno Nettl, and Ronald Byrnside, *Contemporary Music and Musical Cultures* (Englewood Cliffs, N.J., 1975).

Chapter XII

Folk Music and the Composer

A scholarly survey of the uses of folk music in cultivated music is Walter Wiora, *Europäische Volksmusik und abendländische Tonkunst* (Kassel, 1957). A famous composer's view is presented in Ralph Vaughan Williams, *National Music* (London, 1959).

   The treatment of folk music by composers of art music is discussed in most histories of nineteenth- and twentieth-century Western music. See particularly Paul Henry Lang, *Music in Western Civilization* (New York, 1941); Rey M. Longyear, *Nineteenth-Century Romanticism in Music* (Englewood Cliffs, N.J., 1969); and Eric Salzman, *Twentieth-Century Music: An Introduction* (Englewood Cliffs, N.J., 1967), particularly Chapter 8. For American music specifically, see H. Wiley Hitchcock, *Music in the United States: A Historical Introduction* (Englewood Cliffs, N.J., 1969); and Gilbert Chase, *America's Music*, 2nd ed. (New York, 1966), especially Chapters 19 and 20.

INDEX

Page references to song texts and musical examples are in italics.

178

Bruno Nettl is professor of music and anthropology and chairman, Division of Musicology, University of Illinois at Urbana-Champaign. Helen Myers is a graduate student in the Department of Music, Columbia University in the City of New York.

Cover design is by Richard Kinney and the book layout is by Richard Kinney and Judy Mussel. The typeface is Caledonia designed by W. A. Dwiggins in 1940. The display type is Optima designed by Hermann Zapf about 1958.

The text is printed on Mead paper. The hardcover edition is bound in Permalin Buckram cloth over binders' boards; and the paperback edition is perfect bound in CIS enamel cover. Manufactured in the United States of America.